B Margaret,
Thanks for all the help.
Gordon

COMPUTING
NEXT

How the cloud opened the future

GORDON HAFF

Many of the designations used by manufacturers and sellers referred to in this book are claimed as trademarks.

The author has taken care in the preparation of this book, but makes no expressed or implied warranty of any kind and assumes no responsibility for errors or omissions. No liability is assumed for incidental or consequential damages in connection with or arising out of the use of the information contained herein.

This book uses Palatino Linotype and Gill Sans MT typefaces (and an Interstate variant for the cover).

ISBN-13: 978-1481807258
ISBN-10: 1481807250
First version, February 2013.

About the author

Gordon Haff is cloud evangelist for Red Hat, the leading provider of commercial open source software. He is a frequent speaker at customer and industry events. He also writes extensively on and develops strategy for Red Hat's portfolio of open hybrid cloud solutions.

Prior to Red Hat, as an IT industry analyst, Gordon wrote hundreds of research notes, was frequently quoted in publications such as *The New York Times* on a wide range of IT topics, and advised clients on product and marketing strategies. Earlier in his career, he was responsible for bringing a wide range of computer systems, from minicomputers to large Unix servers, to market while at Data General. Gordon has engineering degrees from MIT and Dartmouth and an MBA from Cornell's Johnson School of Management.

He lives west of Boston, Massachusetts in apple orchard country and is an active hiker, skier, sea kayaker, and photographer. He can be found on Twitter as @ghaff, on Google+ as Gordon Haff, and by email at gordon@alum.mit.edu.

Acknowledgements

This book is the product of countless conversations, conferences, briefings, meetings, strategy discussions, and gab sessions with clients, customers, industry acquaintances, friends, and co-workers while at Red Hat and during my time as an industry analyst. That said, any opinions I express in this book are mine alone and should not be taken as statements made on behalf of Red Hat or anyone else —official, unofficial, or otherwise.

Some chapters in this book are adapted, to greater or lesser degrees, from material I wrote previously, including CNET Blog Network posts, Illuminata research, and both credited and uncredited Red Hat publications. I thank the many people who have been involved in any aspect of editing, providing feedback for, and publishing that source material. I would like to especially thank Jonathan Eunice for his insight and editing while I was at Illuminata.

A number of individuals agreed to let me include pieces they have written as chapters in this book. This expert commentary helps provide readers with unique perspectives on a variety of technical and business issues. These pieces have only been lightly edited; where I felt additional context was needed on some point (perhaps because an original blog post contained links), I have added footnotes. These contributors are:

- Bryan Che, James Labocki, and Mark Little of Red Hat
- Andi Mann of CA
- James Urquhart of enStratus
- Michael Coté of Dell
- Judith Hurwitz of Hurwitz and Associates

Other chapters are adapted from interviews with Richard Morrell, Chris Wells, and Matt Hicks of Red Hat. Four steps to building a cloud is adapted, in part, from papers written by Kurt Milne of the IT Process Institute for Red Hat.Finally, I would like to thank Jonathan Gondelman for helping to edit the manuscript.

To my Dad.

For showing me the world,
my education, and everything else.

Table of Contents

Introduction

For the first decade of the 21st century, I was an Information Technology industry analyst. We analysts were different from the Wall Street sort. Rather than trying to predict company stock prices and earning, we were essentially purveyors of advice. We proffered this advice about purchases and technology trends to "users." (A former colleague once remarked that IT is the only industry that borrows the parlance of drug dealers when talking about its customers.) We also advised vendors—those who made the hardware and wrote the software—about how to market and sell to users; said vendors having apparently created such complexity that, more or less uniquely across the commercial landscape, they require ongoing advice about how to navigate their own industry.

In this role, I heard much new terminology and saw many new technologies tentatively advanced—often as trial balloons. It was in the mid-2000s, as the industry reconstituted itself from the bursting of the dot-com bubble, that I saw cloud computing pop up in such a fashion.

The cloud computing thought arose from the large shared services growing on the Internet. Some services, like Google and Facebook, were known by almost everyone. Others, like Amazon Web Services, were mostly known and used by techies. However, over the next five years or so, cloud computing gained such a buzz that the term grew to at least touch upon many of the big ideas happening in computing. The cynical and self-interested called this "cloudwashing." Most everyone else shrugged, maybe bemoaned the imprecision, and got back to doing interesting things that the new technologies coming together made possible.

Think of this book as a linked series of vignettes about cloud computing's past, present, and future. Some of these vignettes are more technical than others, but you can mostly pick and choose where you'd like to dive in. It begins with perspectives on how cloud computing arrived where it is today. As an analyst, I always believed in providing historical context given that so many of today's trends are reinventions or reimaginings of trends past. Nowhere is this truer than in cloud computing.

Next up is openness in clouds. For all the possibilities it creates, cloud computing also creates potentially new vendor control points. But openness isn't just about open source—although open source is part of it. Openness is about everything from communities to interfaces. Cloud, like so much of the modern computing world, is very much a child of the open source model and everything associated with it.

Next, we get more nuts-and-bolts about a hybrid cloud management architecture able to encompass both computing resources at public cloud providers and an organization's own IT department. I also offer some strategies for transitioning from a traditional IT approach to a more services-oriented cloud one.

Operating a cloud covers the need for well-defined operational practices and systems management, as well as what security and risk mitigation really mean in a cloud context.

Cloud computing is also about the developer. Platform-as-a-Service opens up new possibilities for enterprise application development. I describe the rise of PaaS and why customized applications are as important as ever.

Finally, cloud computing is still just part of a broader landscape. Indeed, one of the reasons that cloud computing has garnered so much attention is that its convergence with data and mobility trends in particular is something of a self-reinforcing perfect storm.

It's a storm that is changing the contours of computing.

Gordon Haff
Lancaster, MA
February 2013

The Cloud Turns On

Cloud computing has evolved at a frenetic pace. As a result, cloud computing "1.0" has only a passing resemblance to the cloud computing wave currently shaping the future of the IT landscape. Furthermore, while cloud computing in a sense "reimagines" past antecedents, changes in circumstance and technology mean that the future will not merely be the past warmed over.

The Utility

When I first heard the words "cloud computing," I was probably sitting in my office, then in Nashua, New Hampshire—the heart of old New England manufacturing country. An appropriate locale, as we shall see. Sitting on the third floor of a former textile mill, I could peer down at the Nashua River as it meandered down the center of what had been a thriving Industrial Revolution-era manufacturing city.

Not that this was the first time I had heard the term "cloud" applied to computing. In an earlier life, when I was involved with marketing big business computers of a sort that would later become known as servers, "cloud" was a convenient shorthand for the stuff that happened in the various networks that computers used to talk to each other. We used "cloud" as a term to encompass all the complicated telecommunications technology and associated acronyms that we computer people didn't especially understand—and that, in truth, was mostly irrelevant detail as far as our daily job was concerned.

However, cloud computing as it sprang onto the pages of the tech press around 2006 was something more specific. Google's then-CEO Eric Schmidt is often credited with popularizing the term. As is so often the case with technology, though, the related concepts had been germinating for decades. In a 1961 speech given to celebrate MIT's centennial, artificial intelligence pioneer John McCarthy introduced the idea of a computing utility.

And a utility is what this iteration of cloud computing discussions took as its model.

As recounted by, among others, Nick Carr in his book *The Big Switch*, the utility take on cloud computing metaphorically mirrored the evolution of power generation and distribution. Industrial Revolution factories in the late nineteenth century, such as the one in which I then sat, built largely customized systems to run looms and other automated tools, powered by water or steam turbines.

These power generation and distribution systems were a competitive differentiator; the more power you could produce, the more machines you could run, and the more goods you could manufacture for sale. Today, by contrast, power in the form of electricity is just a commodity for most companies—something to be pulled off the grid and paid for based on how much is used.

The Big Switch argued that computing is on a similar trajectory. You could compute by, in effect, flipping on a light switch: an almost subconscious act that tapped into a reliable, standardized grid of computing efficiently operated by specialists.

If one takes this metaphor at face value, the implications would indeed be extraordinary. The Industrial Revolution-era factory was defined by its customized power systems. My office overlooking the Nashua River was just upstream of a dam, which existed because the energy unleashed by falling water could turn turbines. Rotating turbines, in turn, transmitted power through complex systems of gears and belts, to all manner of factory equipment.

I was also way up on the third floor for a reason. Factories today tend to be expansive, low affairs. That's not an arbitrary decision. It's much easier to move raw materials and finished goods—to say nothing of large and heavy manufacturing equipment—horizontally through a factory than vertically. However, power transmitted mechanically is largely limited by total distance, regardless of whether up, down, or sideways. This both limited the total size of factories and forced them to grow into the air, whatever the other disadvantages.

New England factories tended to favor water power because of the many fast-moving streams and rivers that flow through the area. Rivers now enjoyed by whitewater paddlers are littered with the remains of old dams and other constructions built to create elaborate water power generation systems. By increasing the distance that water falls in one location, dams could multiply the natural power of a river, which was then harnessed through all manner of sluices and flumes.

Power was therefore the product of a highly customized and differentiated infrastructure. A good location and the right design of a "power plant" to best leverage that location was as much a competitive advantage as anything within the factory itself.

Steam turbines came earlier to other regions, such as England, which lacked the hilly topography of New England. In this case, access to coal for the steam turbine boilers helped make some regions particularly attractive for manufacturing. However, the same basic concepts applied. If you ran a factory, power was a big deal.

Electricity, on the other hand, can be sent through wires to motors attached to individual pieces of machinery. There are thousands of motors in a modern manufacturing plant ranging from those in huge gantry cranes to numerous small ones in power tools. There's no need for complex arrays of belts and pulleys, rather than efficient workflows, to dictate the arrangement of factories. As a result, although the changeover was slow at first because of the initial expense and the novelty of electric power, factories began to switch to electricity in earnest during the first decade of the twentieth century. Nick Carr writes that "By 1905, a writer for *Engineering* magazine felt comfortable declaring that 'no one would now think of planning a new plant with other than electric driving.' In short order, electric power had gone from exotic to commonplace."

During this same period, Thomas Edison was putting together the infrastructure to illuminate cities with electric lights. He built the first such infrastructure on Pearl Street in lower Manhattan. On September 4, 1882, Edison switched on his Pearl Street generating station's electrical power distribution system, which provided 110 volts direct current (DC) to 59 customers in lower Manhattan.

While Edison did create an electricity distribution system, his approach was essentially to replace central gasworks utilities with electric ones within the same localized area. And, in fact, his approach using DC effectively limited his distribution network to relatively short distances. By contrast, the competing alternating current (AC) pioneered by George Westinghouse based on Nikola Tesla's research could be transmitted over long distances at high voltages, using lower current (for greater efficiency) and then conveniently stepped down to low voltages for use in homes and factories.

After a long litigious "War of the Currents," the AC system won out. Nevertheless, Tesla's work fell into relative obscurity after his death although he's always been held in high regard by the engineering community — the high-voltage Tesla coil is also named after him. He's even had something of a pop culture comeback in recent years.

The shift of electricity generation from distributed plants to large centralized ones enabled by AC has had a lasting impact. Centralized power generation's advantages improved further as it became possible to build larger and larger turbines. And the coverage spread as the countryside electrified. Today, companies don't generate their own electricity except, perhaps, for backup purposes or to take advantage of some local source of relatively inexpensive power.[1] They don't need to: they just get it off the grid.

Electricity, at least to a first approximation, is no longer custom nor is it a differentiator. It's standardized and a utility.

---

[1] For example, the BMW plant in Spartansburg, South Carolina. uses methane from a nearby landfill to generate over 30 percent of its electricity.

Imagine computing as the new electricity

Until recently, we've been living in an era in which the pendulum has clearly swung in favor of distributed computing. Computers increasingly migrated from the "glass house" of IT out to the workgroups, small offices, and desktops on the periphery. Even before Intel and Microsoft became early catalysts for this trend's exponential growth, computers had been dispersing to some degree for much of the history of computing. The minicomputer and Unix revolutions were among the earlier waves headed in the same general direction.

Whether centralized or decentralized, none of this computing looked very utility-like. The only real question was whether it was the keepers of the systems in the backroom or the users of the systems in the front office who needed to customize and care for their charges. Certainly, no one would confuse operating a computer with flicking on a light switch.

In one sense, our current era is experiencing just another wave : let's call it the mobile wave, or the pervasive wave. Computers are everywhere, from cellphones to MP3 players to refrigerators. But there's a critical difference from the Wintel[2] (and then Linux) wave that ushered in truly widespread distributed computing, including our new mobile wave.

Yes, today the computers that most individuals touch are ubiquitous, but they're increasingly devices for interacting with information generated and stored elsewhere. Or they're autonomous actors handling low-level tasks unbidden. In short, they're conceptually

---

[2] Which is to say, computer systems using Intel microprocessors running the Microsoft Windows operating systems. Over time, competition for the volume market grew with the Linux operating system and microprocessors from Advanced Micro Devices (and more recently, ARM-based designs). But the basic shift from "Big Iron" to smaller and less expensive distributed systems has continued.

more like terminals [3] —albeit compact, sophisticated, mobile ones—than the personal computers of the last wave. Also like terminals, they're mostly simple to use.

PCs went a step further than offering users control over some processing power. They also handed users full control over their data and when and how they connected and interacted with others. Today, by contrast, most of the intelligence is in the network or, more precisely, in the vast server back-end that feeds all these devices.

One face of the Internet's evolution may be the social application running on the cellphone. But the other is the mega-datacenter pulling massive power from the hydroelectric dams on the Columbia River in Washington state. More and more cycles and more and more bits are moving online. Consumer services from Google to Flickr are in the vanguard, but hosted complete applications, à la Salesforce.com, the ubiquitous enterprise sales and marketing tool, are making steady inroads in business as well.

There are security, privacy, and control concerns. The trend is particularly worrisome to folks who embraced distributing computing, i.e. the classic PC, not just as a good technical approach to leveraging the power of cheap microprocessors, but as a good social architecture that puts the user in control of his information and data. Put simply, distributed computing gave users Freedom.

But there are also profound implications for how computers will be built and who will build them—in short, the structure of the whole industry.

Suppose there were just a dozen or half-dozen mega-service providers running mega-datacenters located where a communications nexus can enjoy cheap power. These organizations might have names such as Google or Microsoft. No doubt some countries would get into the game as well. Now here's the question. How would such entities

---

[3] For those below a certain age, think of terminals as essentially like monitors, stupidly displaying whatever they're instructed to do so by the computer to which they're connected.

relate to the today's vendor landscape? Would they still be merely large consumers of processors, servers, and software in much the same vein that they are today?

No. As the largest of these service providers sought competitive differentiation and advantage, it would be very tempting for them to explore custom software and hardware angles that would leave them looking more and more like today's sophisticated hardware systems companies.

We see examples. Google doesn't design or manufacture microprocessors or other silicon, but it does source special parts from Intel that it uses to build many of its own computers. In short, Google already intensely customizes "off-the-shelf" components to its own purposes.

That a company like Google doesn't do even more than this reflects how today's IT world is a world of specialization. No one can "go it alone" to the same degree as the early mainframers or minicomputer makers, who built literally everything from silicon to application software. It's a question of modern complexity and associated economies of scale. Even if Google were to find it could benefit from using some custom "Google search processor," it would almost certainly have it designed and fabricated by someone in the business of doing such things.

But the new scale of re-centralized computing brings different needs, which will, in turn, drive different decisions about building and buying. It's inevitable that Google and its ilk will do many things — whether in-house or through contractors — that independent hardware and software vendors have long become accustomed to thinking their purview. For all intents and purposes, the biggest service providers could become *de facto* system makers (and ones in the old, proprietary, vertically integrated mold). The only difference is that they would take the computing power directly to their customers rather than bothering with the old messy intermediate process of shipping computers that had to be installed, loaded with software, and configured.

In short, the whole landscape of computing would look vastly changed.

The causes of scale

What factors might lead to such mega-scale businesses relative to the computing world of today?

One strong candidate is network effects.

The basic idea behind network effects is that something gets more valuable as more people use it. The canonical example is the telephone system. One lonesome telephone is useless. A few, only mildly interesting. Near-universal connectivity, extremely powerful.

During the past few decades, many of us have seen this pattern applied to email.

I first had access to email in an MIT lab about 1978. It was neat. I occasionally traded emails with a friend of mine, Bert Halstead, who worked at the MIT Artificial Intelligence Lab, about logistics associated with getting to ice hockey scrimmages. But because I didn't know anyone else on email, it wasn't really especially useful.

Flash forward to the late-1980s. I had email at work, but it was a closed system. My company, Data General, had an internal Comprehensive Electronic Office (CEO) setup, a "business automation" package that we sold to customers such as the US Forest Service when such an idea was still pretty new. My personal email was through Compuserve, one of the original commercial online services. I used it a bit, but it wasn't especially handy for things like organizing hiking trips or meetings for a non-profit board I chaired because only a few people in those groups belonged to those network islands. I had to resort to snail mail and telephone anyway. The sea change came when enough people were on interoperable email that I could start treating it as the preferred and default communications medium. Over time, backup communications methods became more and more deprecated until pretty much everyone had to be on email.

This effect can apply to individual companies as well. Some large Internet businesses are clearly network businesses. One great example is eBay, especially when its business primarily revolved around individuals selling used stuff to other individuals. It was the flea market of the Internet and network effects ruled. If I'm looking to buy 19th century maps of Boston, a marketplace with a few hundred or even thousand of sellers is probably not going to be large enough. But eBay was.

Facebook, LinkedIn, and Twitter are among today's canonical examples. In fact, with some caveats, these examples suggest that among social networks of a given type and demographic, there's a winner-take-all effect.

But network effects aren't behind every example of magnitude in the Internet economy. If I were the only person using Google, Google founders Larry Page and Sergey Brin wouldn't be flying around in a private Boeing 767. But, revenue and profits aside, Google doesn't inherently depend on having lots of users to deliver quality results. To be sure, the myriad creators of Web content and the links within that content make Google's PageRank possible, but this is a weak form of network effect compared to the other examples.

Network effects, however, aren't the only reason why a given industry may end up with just a few—or even one—large players. In a 2008 blog post, Nick Carr listed a few that may be relevant to Google and other cloud computing suppliers:

Capital intensity. Building a large utility computing system requires lots of capital, which itself presents a significant barrier to entry.

Scale advantages. Big players reap important scale economies in equipment, labor, real estate, electricity, and other inputs.

Diversity factor. One of the big advantages of utilities is their ability to make demand flatter and more predictable (by serving a diverse group of customers with varying demand patterns), which in turn allows them to use their capital more efficiently. As your customer base expands, so does your diversity factor and hence your efficiency advantage. You then have the ability to undercut your less-efficient competitors' prices.

Expertise advantages. Brilliant computer scientists and engineers are scarce.

Brand and marketing advantages. They still matter—a lot—and they probably matter most of all when it comes to the purchasing decisions of large, conservative companies.

Proprietary systems that create some form of lock-in. Don't assume that "open" systems are attractive to mainstream buyers simply because of their openness. As IT analyst James Governor notes: "customers always vote with their feet, and they tend to vote for something somewhat proprietary—see Salesforce APEX and iPhone apps for example. Experience always comes before open. Even supposed open standards dorks these days are rushing headlong into the walled garden of gorgeousness we like to call Apple Computers."

One interesting thing about this list is that it's not very specific to the IT industry and it's certainly not very specific to cloud computing. Brand, access to capital, and general "throw weight" are all factors that can bestow an advantage on just about any company in just about any industry—unless, of course, size and scale are slowing companies down and keeping them from trying new things quickly. We'll turn to the problems with placing insufficient weight on openness throughout this book.

This bigness/electricity metaphor makes for a spellbinding tale. When the electric utility exploded onto the scene, it changed the design of factories and altered the competitive dynamics of industries. But, does it ultimately apply to this next wave of computing? Is it of a nature that the forces of scale, in whatever combination, will dominate everything else?

But there is no big switch for cloud computing

Greg Papadopoulos was chief technology officer of Sun Microsystems, a company whose CEO was an early and loud popularizer of the computing utility. Papadopoulos, one suspects hyperbolically and with an eye towards something IBM founder Thomas J. Watson probably never said, suggested that "the world only needs five computers," which is to say there would be "more or less, five hyperscale, pan-global broadband computing services giants" each on the order of a Google.[4]

Computing as a new utility is an intriguing and big argument, and one that's been well told. It's also mostly wrong—at least for any time values that we care about as a practical manner.

That doesn't make all the ideas behind cloud computing wrong. This would be a rather short book if that were the case. Computing is getting more network-centric. Check. More standardized. Check. More dynamic. Check. More modular. Check. And so forth.

In fact, I even expect that we will see a rather large-scale shift among small and medium businesses away from running their own e-mail systems and other applications. We've already seen such a shift among consumers; Google search and applications and social media sites are all aspects of cloud computing.

There are economically interesting aspects to this change. No longer do you need to roll in (and finance) pallets of computers to jump-start a company; you can go to the Web site for Amazon Web Services which lets you rent compute capacity, storage space, and other computing services by the hour with no capital outlay. One result is a lower barrier to entry for many types of businesses.

---

[4] As a maker of large, expensive computing hardware that "pan-global broadband services giants" like Google had no particular inclination to buy, it's reasonable to ask why Sun, subsequently gobbled up by database giant Oracle, was pushing this particular agenda. But that's a topic for another day.

But that's not the sort of near-term tectonic shift the electric grid brought about. That grid made both unnecessary and obsolete the homegrown systems of the day. It shifted power generation to large-scale providers and did so relatively quickly.

A shift of that scale won't happen with cloud computing. So far, there is scant evidence that, once you reach the size of industrialized data center operations (call it a couple of data centers to take care of redundancy), the operational economics associated with an order of magnitude greater scale are always going to be a slam dunk.

We see and will see the success of some very large providers like Amazon,[5] Google, and Microsoft. But they won't dominate to the exclusion of everyone else. Nor will we see everything simply move into public clouds of whatever size.

As Rob Livingston, a former CIO at a number of multinational firms, puts it: "The key message here is not to assume that just because it's Cloud it's always going to be cheaper than an on-premise equivalent."

The 2009 study by management consultants McKinsey, "Clearing the Air on Cloud Computing," concluded that outsourcing a typical corporate data center to an Amazon Web Services offering would more than double the cost. As reported in *The New York Times*: "According to McKinsey, the total cost of the data center functions would be $366 a month per unit of computing output, compared with $150 a month for the conventional data center." The article went on to quote Will Forrest, a principal at McKinsey, who led the study: "The industry has assumed the financial benefits of cloud computing and, in our view, that's a faulty assumption."

This McKinsey report was controversial at the time and there's no doubt that cost comparisons between on-premise and off-premise solutions is a tricky business. On the one hand, the cost of maintaining the staff associated with building, managing, securing, hiring the IT specialists, servicing, etc. are rarely all factored into the true cost of

---

[5] If you're only familiar with Amazon as the big Internet store, their Amazon Web Services is also the biggest provider of public cloud services.

computing. On the other hand, outsourcing something is never "fire and forget," especially if you run into unexpected problems with a supplier.

None of this is to suggest that public clouds providers never make sense. In fact, they often do. But the economic argument isn't going to carry the day uncontested.[6]

Furthermore, consider all the reasons businesses, especially large ones, might want or need to continue to run applications in-house (or on a specialist public provider more attuned to their specific needs): control and visibility, compliance with regulations, integration with various existing software and hardware, and so forth.

In short, we should expect a future that is a hybrid of many things, not just one big switch.

These hybrid forms of cloud computing (and the approaches to their creation) will be the topic of much of this book because they are the inevitable future of computing.

---

[6] As we'll get to in a few chapters, I would argue that, for many organizations, public clouds set an objective not impossibly distant but that definitely sets a new benchmark for what the users of internal IT services expect.

What is cloud computing?

If cloud computing isn't "the compute utility" though, what is it?

This turns out to be a question with a less straightforward answer than one might like. For the following reason.

In some computer programming languages, there's a concept called overloading. Without going into the irrelevant technical specifics, this basically means that an "operator" like a + or – sign performs a different function depending upon the context in which it's used. Add 'gordon' + 'haff' and you get 'gordonhaff'. Add 2 + 5 and you get 7. Same operator, conceptually performing the same task ('adding'), but in different ways and with different results depending upon whether words or numbers are involved.

I look at cloud computing similarly. The term has come to mean overlapping but dissimilar things depending on the context. This emphatically does not mean that there's "no there there" other than a bunch of marketing hype.[7] But it does suggest that the cloud consists of several somewhat different threads and encompasses somewhat different things. From my perspective, cloud discussions often conflate at least three different thoughts.[8] I'll try to tease them apart.

The first thread comes closest to the vision of computing as a utility: services delivered at large scale from third-party providers over the Internet. This thread visualizes using computer systems and software owned and operated by others rather than doing so in-house (as was historically the norm).

A service like Google's Gmail is probably what's most familiar to the general public. Rather than a company having to buy a copy of an email program, install it, troubleshoot problems, upgrade it

---

[7] Not that there isn't some of that too.

[8] The cloud computing landscape is more varied still. And I'll get to that. But here I'm not talking about relatively well-defined taxonomies but, rather, discussions taking place at cross-purposes.

periodically, and maintain the computer systems on which it runs, they can just cut a purchase order to Google. There are some ramifications to such a decision—I'll get to those—but it certainly simplifies things. Even if you're renting computing at more of an infrastructure component level[9] for more customized needs than email, we're still talking about moving things that you once needed to own and operate out into the "cloud."

The next thread takes these public cloud concepts as a springboard but adapts them to the needs of individual organizations or communities. These private or hybrid[10] clouds are inspired by public clouds. They graft the operational model of the public cloud onto an IT infrastructure under the control of a single organization. This may reduce costs, but the primary objective is to change the experience of the internal IT user into something more akin to that of someone who presents their credit card to Amazon Web Services and requests storage or compute capacity.

There are many nuances to this aspect of cloud computing. Is a given approach open or locked into a single vendor? How does it relate to server virtualization? Is it about low-level infrastructure like operating systems or is it about a higher level of abstraction? In an environment where users have self-service, how is IT policy expressed and maintained?

A significant chunk of this book will involve these hybrid clouds and their implications. Why they're needed. What "open" means. How they work. Why policy is important.

Finally, cloud computing sometimes gets applied to something very broad—essentially the next generation of information technology.

---

[9] Such as buying number-crunching capacity and storage from Amazon Web Services and writing the software to tie it all together and perform some useful service.

[10] Hybrid is sometimes used narrowly to refer to the combination of a private cloud and a public cloud. However, in this book, I use it is a way that's consistent with the evolving industry meaning to refer to a combination of heterogeneous resources and services wherever they're hosted.

It would be facile to conclude that such a broad definition suggests that cloud computing doesn't, in fact, mean anything at all. On the contrary, we're seeing the convergence of a number of maturing trends—open source, mobility, standardization, virtualization, "big data," modular applications, consumerization—which collectively add up to something that represents a fundamental change in the way that software applications get delivered and consumed. In the final section of this book, I'll take a look at where this "New IT," whether we call it "Open Hybrid Cloud" or something else, is headed. But I will generally restrict my discussion to the changes in the ways in which computing and applications are being managed and delivered to users.

Software, platforms, and infrastructure

The National Institute of Standards and Technology's (NIST) definition, the 16th and final version of which was published in October 2011,[11] is probably the canonical taxonomy of cloud computing. Much of the motivation behind this definition was to standardize US federal government cloud computing procurements; it's hard to compare bids if there's no agreement on vocabulary. However, because the NIST definitions coalesced around a great deal of industry discussion over the course of 15 drafts, it has emerged as a generally accepted framework for cloud computing terminology more broadly.

As we move forward, the limitations of this definition become more and more apparent but it still serves as a useful starting point.

I touched on one way that clouds differ in the last chapter. There are many important distinctions between using public and building private clouds with respect to capital needs and operational requirements. Architecting for hybrid clouds that span multiple locations, technologies, and trust boundaries will be a major theme when we get to a discussion of how we build and operate clouds.

The other major axis on which clouds differ is the co-called service model: XXX-as-a-Service. Essentially, this is the level of abstraction that the service delivers. Three of those levels are spelled out in the NIST definition. Over time, I expect an increasing blending of these models and perhaps a wider acceptance of new ones. For example, authors such as Judith Hurwitz write of "Business Process-as-a-Service" — a higher level of abstraction than mere applications. Nonetheless, at least for today, the NIST definitions are a useful tool to describe the cloud computing landscape.

---

[11] NIST Special Publication 800-145

Software-as-a-Service

SaaS is perhaps the most familiar face of cloud computing. It's the direct use of an application by end-users rather than just by developers or operators. SaaS essentially means hosted applications.

SaaS is arguably orthogonal to other aspects of cloud computing. After all, there is no inherent relationship between the hosted application and the nature of the infrastructure on which it runs. Gmail and Google Apps are SaaS. In the enterprise software space, rather than consumer software realm, the Salesforce.com sales and marketing tool is probably the best known example.

At some point, the distinction between an application and a Website blurs. Are Twitter and Facebook applications? Well, we're more conditioned to call them social networks—which we may access through either a Web browser or an application. We could draw fine distinctions but ultimately we're talking about users doing useful (or fun) things through lightweight interfaces like browsers and smartphone apps. And SaaS is as good an umbrella term as any.[12]

While SaaS is a hugely important part of the evolving software landscape—and I'll discuss it in that vein as I look at the path ahead—it's largely independent of the other aspects of cloud computing covered in this book.

Infrastructure-as-a-Service

IaaS provides building blocks that generally map to concepts familiar to those constructing applications using traditional data center components like virtual machine instances, chunks of data storage, and networks. A user, such as a software developer or system administrator, accesses these resources through a self-service interface —a portal on a Web site.

---

[12] In general we talk of cloud service types as being distinct from whether they run on private, public, or some sort of hybrid infrastructure. SaaS is something of an exception; no one talks about private SaaS; that's just an internally-hosted application or Website.

In a private or hybrid enterprise-administered cloud, these resources will often be provided through a service catalog. A typical item in a service catalog is something like the the operating system, development tools, and supporting software libraries needed to develop mobile applications.

The IaaS approach means that users of the service have granular control over the type of resource they consume and how these various resources are wired together. Subject to any policies that the creator of the service may have put in place, users can make just about any changes they would like. Users can add additional software, update the operating system, use different development tools—but they can't manage or control the underlying compute infrastructure except perhaps select networking configurations or physical location of the resources at a gross geographical level.

On the other hand, users are responsible, to a large degree, for scaling their application and provisioning all the services required to run it. An IaaS makes it easy for an IT shop to offer users, such as developers, self-service compute environments in an automated and repeatable way. But it's the logical equivalent of giving users a server configured with a specific software load; it's general-purpose but it needs to be managed. Developers are responsible for the underlying plumbing that may not be especially relevant to their Web or business analysis application.

Platform-as-a-Service

The PaaS term covers a lot of ground. In a way, it covers everything that's somewhere between an IaaS and a SaaS and those categories also blend into it.

Some of the higher-level public cloud services that Amazon Web Services (AWS) and other public cloud providers offer are really platform rather than base-level IaaS. Think replication or data services that go beyond the basics and are often unique to a specific provider. At the same time, many SaaS providers offer application programming interfaces (APIs) that developers can use to add functions, such as customized reporting or analytics, to the base product. The Force.com ecosystem, which extends the basic Salesforce.com SaaS product is a great illustration of Platform-as-a-Service.

Whatever the specifics though, the basic idea behind a PaaS is that it provides a platform on which a user, often a software developer, can build without having to worry about the details which are unimportant from his perspective anyway. Of course, at some level, everything that serves as a foundation for further building is a platform. However, in this context, platform refers to a higher level of abstraction than an operating system or an operating system plus some basic components (such as a LAMP stack with Linux).

For example, a PaaS may automate common tasks such as scaling applications. It can make sure that various programming language runtimes are present and updated. It may provide redundancy automatically. The basic idea is that a developer wants to code without worrying about the details of how that code executes within an IT infrastructure.

Important early PaaS offerings began life as hosted offerings specific to a single provider and geared towards a single language and set of programming interfaces. An important trend in the PaaS marketplace is an evolution towards a greater emphasis on application portability and choice in programming languages and frameworks (sometimes referred to as "polyglot"). This shift is making PaaS more suitable for enterprises and also makes PaaS more interesting to application architects and system administrators, rather than just developers looking for an easy application development tool.

How evolution begat the cloud revolution

Asking why cloud computing is happening today is something of a tautology. An inclusive definition of cloud computing essentially equates it with a broad swath of the major advances happening in IT today. Even narrower definitions touch on many of the important threads relating to how IT operations, architectures, approaches, and software development are changing.

Pervasive virtualization, fast application and service provisioning, elastic response to changes in user demand, low-touch management, network-centric access, and the ability to move workloads from one location to another are all hallmarks of cloud computing. In other words, cloud can be more of a shorthand for the "interesting stuff going on in IT" — or at least in back-end computing — than it is a specific technology or approach.

But that doesn't make the question meaningless. It would be hard to argue that there isn't a huge amount of excitement (and, yes, hype) around changing the way that we operate data centers, access applications, and deploy new business services. But leaving aside the cloud computing moniker, the question becomes: Why is this broad-based rush to do things differently happening right now?

The answer lies in how largely evolutionary trends can, given the right circumstances, come together in a way that results in something revolutionary.

Take the Internet. ARPANET — the Internet's predecessor — was first established in 1969. Something akin to hypertext, the link you click to go to a Website, was first described by Vannevar Bush in a 1945 article; Apple shipped Hypercard in 1984. But it took the convergence of inexpensive personal computers with graphical user interfaces, faster and more standardized networking, the rise of small inexpensive servers connected together in large numbers, the World Wide Web and the Mosaic browser that talked to it, open source software like Linux and Apache, and the start-up culture of Silicon Valley to usher

27

in the Internet as we know it today. And that convergence, once it began, happened quickly and dramatically.

The same could be said of cloud computing. The following interrelated trends are among those converging to make cloud computing not only possible and interesting, but transformational.

Comfort level with and maturation of mainstream server virtualization. Virtualization, which I'll discuss in more detail, serves as the foundation for several types of cloud computing including public Infrastructure-as-a-Service clouds like Amazon's and most private cloud implementations. But the connection goes beyond technology. Increasingly ubiquitous virtualization has required that IT organizations become comfortable with the idea that they don't know exactly where their applications are physically running. Cloud computing is even more dependent on accepting a layer of abstraction between software and its hardware infrastructure (although, at the same time, it can more completely abstract away underlying complexity).

The build-out of a vendor and software ecosystem alongside and on top of virtualization. From a technology perspective, cloud computing is about the layering of automation tools, including those for policy-based administration and self-service management. From this perspective, cloud computing is the logical outgrowth of virtualization-based services—although it also involves the layering of resource abstraction on top of the hardware abstraction which virtualization provides. Cloud computing can also involve concepts like pay-per-use pricing, but these too have existed in various forms in earlier generations of computing.

Lightweight application access. The corollary of mobile workloads within the datacenter which can move from server to server is the mobility of access devices. Many enterprise applications historically depended on the use of specific client software. In this respect, "client-server" and then PCs were something of a step back compared to applications accessed with just a green-screen terminal. (But, in exchange, this complexity meant that applications could leverage the

28

local computing power and graphics on the "fat client.") Today's trend towards being able to access applications from any Web browser is effectively a prerequisite for the public cloud model and helps make internal IT more flexible as well. Ubiquitous browser-based application access (and the complementary app store approach that began on the smartphone) is one of the big differences between today's hosted software and the Application Service Providers of circa 2000.

Mobility and the consumerization of IT are also driving the move to applications that aren't dependent on a specific client configuration or location. For more than a decade, we've seen an inexorable shift from PCs connected to a local area network to laptops running on Wi-Fi to an increasing diversity of devices such as smartphones and iPads hooked up to all manner of networks. Fewer and fewer of these devices are even supplied by an employer and many are used for both personal and business purposes. All this further reinforces the shift away from dedicated, hard-wired corporate computing assets.

The expectations created by consumer-oriented Web services. The likes of Facebook, Flickr, 37signals, Google, and Amazon (from both Amazon Web Services and e-commerce services perspectives) have raised the bar enormously when it comes to user expectations around ease of use, speed of improvement, and richness of interface. Enterprise IT departments rightly retort that they operate under a lot of constraints—whether data security, detailed business requirements, or uptime—that a free social-media site does not. Nonetheless, the consumer Web sets an expectation and IT departments increasingly find users taking their IT into their own hands when the official solution isn't good enough. This forces corporate IT to be faster and more flexible about deploying new services.

None of these trends really had a single pivotal moment. Arguably, virtualization came closest with the advent of native hypervisors for x86 servers in 2001. But, even there, the foundational pieces dated to IBM mainframes in the 1960s and it took a good decade even after x86 virtualization arrived on the scene to move beyond consolidating lightweight applications, primarily on the Microsoft Windows operating system, to become ubiquitous (although not universal).

Web application richness and the way access to those applications is transforming in a variety of ways (some of which will end up being more viable than others) is also an important trend. The next-generation HTML5 language used on Web pages, browser-centric laptops, smartphones, tablets, TVs that look more like computers, app stores, and higher-performance wireless communications are just a few of the developments that could affect how we access applications and what those applications look like.

Collectively, there's a big change afoot and cloud computing is as good a term for much of it as any. But we got here through largely evolutionary change that has come together into something much bigger.

And that's a good thing. New computing ideas that require lots of ripping and replacing have a generally poor track record. So the fact that cloud computing is in many ways the result of evolution makes it more interesting, not less.

The shipping container and the cloud

The story of the shipping container nicely illustrates how new approaches—even those that are radically new and ultimately transformative—are still rooted in the past in important regards.

The story of the shipping container, as author Marc Levinson described it in *The Box: How the Shipping Container Made the World Smaller and the World Economy Bigger,* illustrates how even ultimately transformative new technologies still proceed naturally out of past developments. The shipping container radically changed the economics of shipping the goods we purchase and use every day. Without the shipping container, the globalization of goods would never have happened—at least not at nearly the scale it has. The container embodies a lot of interesting lessons for how technologies evolve more broadly.

It has lessons about both possibilities and constraints. But also about how practices may have to change in order to realize the potential of new technology.

Existing infrastructure matters. The size of container ships is largely constrained by the width and depth of the Panama and Suez Canals. A "Panamax" container ship is the maximum size that can go through the Panama Canal; a "Suezmax" the largest that can go through the Suez Canal. "Malaccamax" ships have the maximum draught that can traverse the Strait of Malacca. In a totally different context, there's a good argument that the Segway, a much ballyhooed self-balancing "personal transportation vehicle," failed, not so much because of price or poor design, but because it wasn't a good fit with either existing sidewalks or roads (which also remains an issue with widespread bicycle use in most American cities).

Standards matter. Containers have been around in various forms since at least the 1800s, beginning with the railroads. In the U.S., the container shipping industry's genesis is usually dated to Malcom McLean in 1956. However, for about the next twenty years, many shipping companies used incompatible sizes for both containers and the corner fittings used to lift them. This in turn required multiple variations of equipment to load and unload and otherwise made it hard for a complete logistics system to develop. This changed around 1970 when standard size and fittings and reinforcement norms were developed (with all the political jostling between the incumbents that you'd expect).

Process matters. At least as important as standards were changes to the labor agreements at major ports. When containers were first introduced, existing labor contracts negated much of their economic benefit by requiring excess dockworkers or otherwise requiring processes that involved more handling than was actually necessary. For reason of both new labor agreements and infrastructure, containerization allowed the Port Newark-Elizabeth Marine Terminal to largely eclipse the New York and Brooklyn commercial port.

The story of the shipping container has particular relevance to cloud computing. Like the container, the basic concepts aren't new but they are being made more relevant to a wider audience by the maturation of associated infrastructure (such as the network).

Cloud adoption within organizations can certainly be constrained by the infrastructure already in place. An approach which requires dramatic reboots of a business' application and infrastructure portfolio is typically not going to be a workable approach. By the same token, though, increased standardization—even if the resulting infrastructure is still heterogeneous in many respects—makes unified cloud management more approachable. And commonality between these enterprise architectures and those used by public cloud providers similarly make possible hybrid architectures that would have faced almost insurmountable technical challenges in a prior era when incompatible proprietary computer systems were the norm.

Standards will matter—at least to reach the point of interoperable clouds. That the IT industry has increasingly adopted common networking and other standards as it has more standardized computing architectures lays the framework for cloud standards. Standards for cloud computing itself will evolve over time and, as has often been the case in the past, various translation layers and shims will often take the place of full standards-based interoperability — especially in areas where technology is still evolving.

And the business processes are, as always, highly relevant to the computing resources which, after all, are ultimately there to support them. Processes rooted in manual approaches with lots of human back and forth won't see much benefit from new technology no matter how virtualized, service-oriented, or self-service. Human intervention throttles automated processes. This isn't to say that checks and balances aren't needed — but they should mostly be based on automated policy controls with manual intervention and not the norm.

The Amazon model

Most of this book will focus on how organizations can build and manage hybrid clouds. However, given that hybrid spans both the private and public spheres, a cloud like Amazon's is very much part of this equation. Indeed, as we've seen, there remains a school of thought that these public clouds *are* the one and only future. I won't debate that particular point further but merely stipulate that public clouds, in their various forms, are an important part of the present and future of computing. And Amazon is the eight hundred pound gorilla in that space.

By the time that Amazon CEO Jeff Bezos appeared on the cover of Time Magazine as 1999's Person of the Year, Amazon.com had already started to significantly expand beyond its roots as the "world's biggest bookstore." By then it was also selling, not only CDs and movies, but also power tools, toys, televisions, and more. It was also still losing hundreds of millions of dollars per year—a loss that, however fashionable in the dot-com bubble, is still a lot of money. Then, as now, rail-thin margins are a big part of Amazon's financial challenge —especially for the sort of mass-market commodities that make up much of Amazon's business, constrained as they are by the prices charged by both other Web retailers and by brick-and-mortar stores.

As a result, Amazon eyed related and complementary businesses which didn't involve directly selling the tangible "stuff" that Amazon had to inventory and distribute on their own nickel. For example, by 1999, Amazon had started its "zShops" program (which became the "Amazon Marketplace" in 2006)—essentially a complete hosted e-commerce infrastructure for third-party merchants. Amazon's attraction to this sort of business is that it is effectively collecting "tolls" on every transaction processed, while being called on to do little more than provide access to the company's transactional infrastructure. Yes, it's a pricey and complicated infrastructure to setup in the first place. But, at least over time, incremental scale can be added relatively inexpensively.

In 2006, Amazon took this strategy to the next level by introducing a variety of Web services. Some of the services straightforwardly extended and leveraged earlier offerings in e-commerce and search. However, three services—Elastic Compute Cloud (EC2), Simple Storage Service (S3), and Simple Queue Service (SQS)—were pure utility infrastructure offerings. As I wrote in 2007: "While still in quite early days, they suggest that Amazon increasingly sees itself as much about delivering just the electrons as the complete atoms."

A persistent story continues to make the rounds that Amazon Web Services (AWS) was created to effectively lease Amazon's excess computer capacity outside of the November to January holiday season —a period during which, like other retailers, Amazon does much of its business. But this appears to be merely apocryphal. Werner Vogels, Amazon's CTO, has written that "The excess capacity story is a myth. It was never a matter of selling excess capacity, actually within 2 months after launch AWS would have already burned through the excess Amazon.com capacity. Amazon Web Services was always considered a business by itself, with the expectation that it could even grow as big as the Amazon.com retail operation."

Some of the concepts within AWS had existed previously. S3 resembled the storage service providers of the dot-com era. EC2 bore more than a passing resemblance to Sun Microsystem's much-hyped Sun Grid Compute Utility—although that was based on physical servers rather than AWS' virtual infrastructure. But Amazon succeeded where those others had not through a combination of scale, low pricing, embracing new lightweight Web protocols, and an aggressive focus on continually rolling out new services and new capabilities.

It probably didn't hurt either that AWS rolled out around the dawn of the second great Internet boom, which distinguished itself from the first one in part by far less investor appetite for huge outlays of up-front capital. In this startup climate, the availability of cheap pay-per-use compute capacity was extremely attractive.

Whatever the precise reasons, AWS has grown enormously (although nailing down anything approaching exact numbers remains something of a technology press and financial analyst parlor game). As of this writing, the latest estimate from Macquarie Capital pegged AWS' 2013 revenue at $3.8 billion, up from under $1 billion in 2010.

For a more visceral sense of how AWS has grown and how it has engaged with all manner of developers and companies, you couldn't have done better than to attend the AWS Re:Invent conference in Las Vegas right after Thanksgiving 2012. That is, if you could get in. Their first customer and partner conference sold out its 6,000 or so tickets. The level of advancement in just five years or so was striking.

Amazon focused considerable energy on making the case that even the most critical and demanding applications could run on their cloud. One such example was NASDAQ's QMX FinQloud, a cloud computing resource powered by AWS specifically intended for the financial services sector. That said, the conference was also replete with familiar examples of the-usual-suspect mature startup businesses that continue to use AWS almost exclusively. Think movie and TV subscription service Netflix and photo sharing site SmugMug.

Ultimately, consistent with a theme I'll return to again and again in this book, it's not a matter of public clouds not being secure or generally inadequate on any single dimension. It's a matter of suitability of purpose where that suitability is often in the eye of the beholder.

The cloud in the forest

In a 2009 blog post, longtime IBMer Irving Wladawsky-Berger offered a good way to think about the evolution toward cloud computing.

> We should view computing models much more like forests than trees. These computing model forests have a variety of different trees, and the transition between them is gradual, not abrupt. With the passage of time, as you walk around them you begin to see new trees, but the old ones are still around. But one day you realize that the forest you are now walking through is markedly different from the one you were in twenty years ago.

Put another way, it's evolutionary rather than revolutionary — neither a new term applied to the same old thing nor an overnight sea change in the way that all computing is done. Terminological debates will doubtless continue, and there are plenty of unanswered questions about exactly which new "trees" will thrive and which will die out. However, we're starting to see some consensus emerge around at least the broad outlines of the cloud's evolution.

As Wladawsky-Berger wrote after a 2009 MIT Sloan CIO Symposium:

> A lot of the benefits of cloud computing, such as virtualization, shared infrastructures, highly disciplined systems management, flexible deployment and scalability are of value to just about all data centers and service providers, whether you run them as a private clouds providing services to only members of the company, or as public clouds open to everyone. There is also general agreement that you should make cloud deployment decisions on a case-by-case basis, especially decisions as to which applications should be run on private versus public clouds. Public cloud deployments make the most sense for highly commoditized, standardized, mass customized applications.

During a panel at the same symposium, there was also a broad consensus that infrastructure savings and flexible scaling were key factors driving the adoption of cloud computing. One panelist remarked that "The benefits of cloud computing start and end with the dollars you can save. But it can also help getting your best people away from working in areas that can be outsourced to the cloud. This way you can allow your best people to focus on an area that drives differentiation for your company."

A few points worth highlighting:

Cloud-like computing architectures within organizations are garnering a lot of interest. Whether you call them "private clouds" or just the next iteration of service-oriented architectures (SOA), the bottom line is that organizations—especially larger ones—are far more interested in leveraging the approaches embodied by cloud computing than they are in actually hosting their applications elsewhere.

There's also interest in the public cloud, but it's often for standard off-the-shelf applications in the form of hosted applications, Software-as-a-Service (SaaS), or certain types of new applications. This is, in fact, wholly consistent with the established pattern of IT outsourcing. Payroll was perhaps the first application to be farmed out in a widespread way. Important? Sure. But also largely standardized and in no way a source of competitive advantage. New applications—though not all—will better align with new types of infrastructure as well.

Distractions matter. Enterprises can arguably do a lot of things as cheaply in-house as can a third-party. However, a corporation also runs the risk of keeping too many plates spinning at any one time. Ultimately businesses need to focus on their core competencies and concerns.

It's arguably been the dramatic "Big Switch" take on cloud computing with which I introduced this section that has led to so much of the cloud hype. But it's the enabling technologies—as adopted in thousands of distributed organizations—that are more relevant for any reasonable planning horizon.

And that's a good segue because hybrid clouds are where a lot of action in cloud computing is taking place today. But, first, open source and everything associated with it has played such a large role in today's computing world that a brief detour is in order.

Open Clouds

Openness and open source weave into many of this book's topics. Some brief background is in order. This is by no means a detailed history of "free software," open source, the philosophical underpinnings of the movement, the companies and individuals who played major parts, how it works as a development process, or a thorough examination of legal subtleties. Rather, the intent is to help you understand the practical ways in which open source intersects cloud computing.

Whence open source. *There are many misconceptions about open source even by people who are otherwise very familiar with the software industry. As a result, I'm going to spend some time tracing the history of open source and show how it came to its present predominant position.*

Communities over free-riders. *The ways in which thinking about open source licenses has evolved over time.*

How cloud changes the rules (or not). *Open source software licensing grew up in a world of technical constraints and conditions which might initially seem to have little to do with cloud computing. But open source and other aspects of openness very much do.*

What makes a cloud open. *Open source was a means to an end in a world where computer systems running unique operating systems and applications were the norm. Open source remains important in a world in which hardware and operating systems are more standardized even as the locales where a given application may run are more varied. But many more factors come into play as well.*

Whence open source

Consider the evolution of open source through the lens of the operating system.

The first computers didn't even have operating systems—of which today's open source Linux is one of the most popular examples. Users ran programs that controlled the entire machine and explicitly told the hardware how to perform calculations or do other tasks. The first operating system is generally considered to be the GM-NAA I/O system created in 1956 by Bob Patrick of General Motors and Owen Mock of North American Aviation for the IBM 704 mainframe. A lot of things were left as an exercise for the users in the early days. GM-NAA I/O, its successors like SHARE, and other early OSs were all written by customers.

Operating systems evolved to provide an increasingly rich set of services to applications so they didn't have to reinvent the wheel. One important aspect of these services was that they remained relatively consistent and stable, at least for major commercial products.[13] Put another way, they constitute a sort of "contract" for applications that run on top. There's effectively a promise that, if you write a program to the defined operating system interfaces, things will still work even if you install a new type of disk or if you double the number of processors. They also insulate applications making use of those services from the hardware and the low-level software that talks directly to hardware. Done right, this abstraction allows innovation to occur in one layer of the hardware/software stack without forcing everything else to change.

Finally, operating systems handle basic processes and memory management so that application programs don't need to worry about the processor on which their instructions are executing, or the specific physical location on a disk drive where their data is stored. That may seem like just-the-way-things-work to the average user who even

---

[13] Indeed, part of the value commercial operating systems (such as Red Hat Enterprise Linux from my employer) offer is consistency within and across versions.

thinks about such things today. But basic process scheduling on multi-processor systems and the many tasks handled by filesystems were once the responsibility of programmers and system operators. Over time, OSs have largely abstracted away those tasks.

In the early days, it was considered something of an innovation if an operating system wasn't tied to a single generation of hardware. Furthermore, many of the operating system functions that we now take for granted had to be performed by applications or by utility programs—if, in fact, the functions were available at all.

Against this background, the Unix operating system developed at Bell Labs, the research arm of the old AT&T, was a bit unusual. Created by Ken Thompson, Dennis Ritchie, and others, Unix—although originally developed in low-level assembly language—was soon rewritten in the higher-level C language partly to simplify developing versions which would run on different types of hardware. The higher-level the language, the less tied to the details of a specific type of hardware.[14]

Under the terms of a 1958 consent degree stemming from one of its ongoing series of antitrust cases, Bell Labs had to license its non-telephone technology to anyone who asked. AT&T did so under under licenses, which included all source code—text files that can be edited and fed through a compiler to create instructions which a computer can use directly.

By the late seventies, Unix was running on all manner of hardware from IBM mainframes to Digital Equipment Corporation minicomputers (and many more besides). Access to the source code allowed licensees themselves, rather than AT&T, to do much of the work required to "port" Unix to all these varied hardware architectures.

---

[14] Using higher-level computer languages and other types of abstraction usually trade off some degree of efficiency for ease of development and operation. Computer memory and performance were still at very much a premium in the early seventies, making the use of a high-level language for this purpose at least somewhat controversial.

One of the educational licensees, the University of California, Berkeley, modified and added features to its licensed version of Unix and, in 1978, began shipping those add-ons as the Berkeley Software Distribution (BSD). Over time, BSD added many new features and came to be viewed as a substantially different product from that shipped by AT&T. In fact, in 1988, Berkeley would eventually release a version of BSD, Networking Tape 1 (Net/1), that no longer contained any of the original AT&T code and therefore didn't require an AT&T license. Instead, Berkeley made it freely redistributable under the terms of its own BSD license, which as we'll see is a particularly permissive open source license. AT&T would subsequently sue Berkeley for copyright infringement but the suit was settled largely in Berkeley's favor in 1994.

In parallel with the commercial growth of Unix, Richard Stallman was working in the MIT Artificial Intelligence (AI) lab where he became convinced that people needed to be able to freely modify the software that they used. In 1985, Stallman published the GNU Manifesto, which outlined his motivation for creating a free operating system called GNU, which would be "compatible"[15] with Unix. The name GNU is a recursive acronym for "GNU's Not Unix."

To this day, there is no "GNU operating system" in that the GNU Hurd operating system kernel has never been completed. However, Stallman did complete many components of his operating system. These included, critically, the parts needed to build a functioning operating system from source code as well as utilities such as a text editor. They were licensed under a "copyleft" license, the General Public License (GPL), which required that, when software is distributed, the source code, including any changes made, be distributed as well. (By contrast, the BSD license does not impose this requirement; it's therefore often described a a "permissive" license.)

Because Unix has always had a relatively modular design, it was possible to combine the working GNU components with a kernel from

---

[15] "Compatible" is a rather complicated and loaded word in the context of Unix but it's the word used by Stallman in his manifesto.

somewhere else. That kernel, called Linux, was developed by a Finnish college student named Linus Torvalds, working on and inspired by MINIX, a minimal version of Unix written by Andrew Tanenbaum to teach computer science.[16] (MINIX was effectively used to bootstrap the development of the new kernel, a common practice for new operating systems.) In August 1991, he posted news of his project to the Internet newsgroup comp.os.minix, inviting feedback and suggestions. Linux development, under Stallman's GPL license, continued throughout the Nineties. By the time of the Internet boom in the latter half of the decade, Linux had leveraged the open source development model to emerge as the standard infrastructure software for the Internet age.

I've presented this history to show how open source software as we know it today is, in important respects, the product of the environment from which it first sprang. The setting was largely academic (University of California, Berkeley in the case of BSD Unix, and MIT in the case of the GPL) and the operating system platform was largely Unix or Unix-like derivatives.

I've only touched on the long and twisted history of Unix' genesis at Bell Labs, its growth into a commercial operating system, and the subsequent Unix wars. But suffice it to say that a number of historical factors greatly influenced what we usually think of as open source today:

- Throughout the early history of Unix, source code was widely available and widely-shared. For example, large chunks of mid-Seventies vintage Sixth Edition Unix became widely available in *samizdat* fashion; and were eventually published in the well-known book *Lion's Commentary on UNIX 6th Edition* (though the book was published with the right to use the code for educational purposes only).

---

[16] Strictly speaking, Linux therefore refers only to the operating system kernel although it's widely used to refer to complete distributions of Linux plus all manner of associated programs and utilities. Some purists push the term "GNU/Linux" although this has never been widely accepted.

- During the 1980s, the mechanisms to exchange files and communicate through email and newsgroups was fairly commonplace in the computer science departments at places like Berkeley and MIT (which were connected to the Internet's precursor) while they were still relatively unknown in the broader world.

- Unix was designed as a portable operating system that could run on a wide range of incompatible hardware platforms, but had to be modified to do so.

Thus, this culture had a history of sharing source code and the mechanisms to share source code and work on it collaboratively. This access to source code turned out to be very useful because you needed it to port programs to all the varied operating system flavors, processor architectures, and hardware designs out there.

"Software Freedom" therefore focused on viewing, modifying, and redistributing source code —often with license terms that reflected specific technical aspects of a Unix environment—because the source code and the right to run it were what mattered most. The ideological underpinnings of the Software Freedom movement are not really about open source *per se* but, historically, open source was the practical mechanism to achieving the greatest degree of freedom.

Communities over free-riders

Historically, talk open source, and people have tended to focus on the source code and the license.

Some licenses are essentially legacy licenses; in general, the continued proliferation of licenses has abated in recent years but it's often more trouble than it's worth to retire licenses that are still in use by active software. Others won't be relevant to a specific type of copyrighted material, such as software programs. (Material under an open source license is still copyrighted; indeed, copyright law is integral to the working of open source licensing.)

However, when it comes to open source software licenses specifically, there are two broad categories. One includes "copyleft" licenses, of which the General Public License (GPL) is the best known. (The Linux operating system uses the GPL.) The other includes "permissive" licenses, most notably the Apache, BSD, and MIT licenses.

Different licenses impose more, fewer, or different types of restrictions within that general framework. But those two categories capture the core philosophical distinction.[17] A copyleft license requires that if changes are made to a program's code, and the changed program is distributed outside an organization, the source code containing the changes must likewise be distributed. Permissive licenses don't.

Among newer projects, there's a general trend towards greater use of more permissive licenses. Matthew Aslett of market researcher 451 Group wrote in 2011 that: "2010 was the first year in which there were more companies formed around projects with non-copyleft licenses than with strong copyleft licenses." Other data shows a similar trend, as do the anecdotal observations of industry observers.

---

[17] A class of licenses are copyleft at the level of individual source code files, rather than the program as a whole. This is arguably an important distinction even if the reality is that these licenses, of which Mozilla Public License is the best-known example, aren't in especially broad use today.

My take is that this shift reflects less concern about preventing free-riders and more concern about growing communities. The Eclipse Foundation's Ian Skerrett puts it this way: "I claim all these projects use a permissive license to get as many users and adopters, to encourage potential contributions. They aren't worried about trying to force anyone. You can't force anyone to contribute to your project; you can only limit your community through a restrictive license."

Or to put it another way, open source is no longer widely viewed as a child that needs to be protected.

Today, open source is widely embraced by all manner of technology companies because they've found that, for many purposes, open source is a great way to engage with developer and user communities —and even with competitors. It's emerged as a great model for developing software and capturing innovation wherever it's happening.

Therefore, the concern that, left to their own devices, companies will wholesale strip-mine open-source projects and "take it all private" seems anachronistic. That's not to say that it will never happen or that everyone will always contribute as much code without copyleft as with it, but the suggestion that copyleft is all that's holding the whole open-source process together just doesn't square with the facts.

As a result, more people are now approaching licensing pragmatically, rather than ideologically.

The adoption of the new version of the GPL, GPLv3, in late 2007 is illustrative. The prior version of the license is used by Linux and many other open source projects. Updating it was a long, loud, and contentious process. But after all the *sturm und drang*, it's now unclear what real impact the GPLv3 will have. Depending upon whom you ask, clauses concerning ideological sticking points such as digital rights management were either narrowed in scope or de-fanged completely. And it seems possible—probable even—that Linux, perhaps the best-known open source project licensed under the GPL, will never move to the new license version.

More broadly, there just doesn't seem to be a whole lot of interest, much less passion, out there in the various open source communities for fighting license battles. That's not to say that everyone agrees that there is one perfect approach to licensing. Not at all! But there is, for the most part, a pragmatic understanding and a realization that the license for a given open source project has to match up with its governance, collaboration, and even business model. It's just one piece of the puzzle.

Bet on the Community, Not the Current State of Technology by Bryan Che

An example of the importance of community is offered here in the context of OpenStack, an open source Infrastructure-as-Service project that has been

buoyed by huge developer and other community interest and the establishment of an independent OpenStack Foundation.[18] *Bryan Che is co-General Manager of Red Hat's Cloud Business Unit. Adapted from http://tentenet.net/2012/08/13/ the-2nd-tenet-of-open-source-bet-on-the- community-not-the-current-state-of-technology/, originally published August 2012.*

Unix or Linux of Cloud?

I recently spoke with an analyst who asked me about Marten Mickos' comment at GigaOm Structure that "OpenStack, rather than following in Linux' footsteps, could become 'the Unix of cloud.' The implication was that so many vendors weighing in could lead to a forking or fracturing of the OpenStack standard."[19] Similarly, many others have recently been asking if OpenStack would become the "Linux of Cloud?"

No, the Linux of Cloud is Linux. However, the thrust behind either of these questions essentially boils down to: When evaluating open source technologies for cloud, how do you pick a winner? How do you know if a project is going to succeed like Linux or fracture and decline like Unix?

---

[18] CloudStack, another open source IaaS project, has also likely has benefited from its shift to being governed by the Apache Software Foundation rather than by its primary sponsor, Citrix.

[19] This comment refers to the infamous "Unix wars" that resulted in the proliferation of many incompatible versions of Unix, a topic which (thankfully) is beyond the scope of this book.

The answer is the 2nd Tenet of Open Source: Bet on the Community, Not the Current State of Technology.

Why Linux Succeeded

I joined Red Hat back in 2002 before we first released Red Hat Enterprise Linux (RHEL). I can tell you—and no one at Red Hat will dispute this—that RHEL was inferior to Solaris and other Unix variants in many ways back then. So, how were we able to succeed with RHEL, and why has Linux won against Unix? We had three things going for us:

- An unbeatable value combination of open source software on commodity x86 hardware

- A Linux distribution that enterprises could trust due to the certification of hardware vendors and ISVs, support, and stable and predictable releases with good lifecycles (RHEL)

- A large and growing open source community driving fast innovation into Linux

The first two features were what earned Red Hat the right to have conversations with enterprises about switching from Unix to Linux. Enterprises were willing to listen to us because of our value and enterprise promises. But, it was this large and diverse open source community that enabled us to win the industry.

Winning With Open Source

If you would have evaluated what operating system to use as the basis of enterprise data centers back in 2002 based on the current state of technology back then, certainly Unix would have won that comparison over Linux. But, Linux had such a large number of contributors and developers across the open source community that its pace of innovation eclipsed what any of the Unix vendors could achieve, and Linux eventually overtook Unix from a capability standpoint.

Consider that even today, Red Hat only has about 5,000 employees. At its height, Sun Microsystems employed over 38,000 employees.

Back in 2002, we only had a few hundred employees. But, in the open source model, Red Hat didn't have to write all the features of Linux. Instead, we had partners like IBM, Intel, HP, Dell, and many others contributing to Linux to optimize and advance it to run on their platforms. Since 2005, just to the Linux kernel alone, the open source community for Linux has included:

- over 15 million lines of code in version 3.2
- over 7,800 developers
- over 800 unique employers

It was the size, diversity, and strength of this open source community that propelled Linux to its leadership position against Unix. Contrast that with Unix, where you had many different vendors each advancing their own proprietary operating systems with no code sharing or common hardware platforms or integrated community. The united Linux community easily advanced Linux past each of these Unix fiefdoms, and the rest is history. Unix started with a much stronger technology base, but Linux's community won in the end.

OpenStack and Open Source

Now, let's consider the current state of OpenStack technology and community. From a technology standpoint, OpenStack has certainly come a long way quite quickly. But, it is not yet widely deployed or more advanced than many other IaaS cloud technologies in the market. And, there are a number of cloud offerings that have been available for much longer than OpenStack has existed, including open source projects like Eucalyptus or cloud.com/CloudStack. Indeed, at Red Hat, we don't think OpenStack is quite enterprise-ready yet for the majority of the market.

But what an open source community OpenStack is building! For its most recent Essex release, OpenStack had some impressive numbers, including:

- 421,695 lines of code added and 256,904 lines of code removed
- 217 developers contributed

- 100 unique employers contributed

No, these aren't yet at the scale of Linux, but they are clearly a sign of a rapidly growing and healthy community. In fact, with the announcement earlier this spring that OpenStack is finally moving to an open governance structure, Red Hat joined the new OpenStack foundation as a platinum member. And we aim to provide the same combination of value, enterprise-class distribution, and rapid open source development in OpenStack that we did for Linux.

So, what is the effect of OpenStack's large open source community? Is it hurting OpenStack and devolving it into the Unix of tomorrow compared with other open source cloud technologies? Google Trends, though by no means a definitive prophet, offers an interesting view. Compare OpenStack, Eucalyptus, Cloud.com, and CloudStack. What's the difference between these different open source projects? OpenStack has the largest open source community.

Betting on OpenStack

Today, Red Hat announced the availability of its preview release of our upcoming Red Hat OpenStack product. Why just a preview and not a full product yet? We are currently in the process of bringing the same value proposition to OpenStack that we have done for Linux and many other open source products, from JBoss middleware to Red Hat Enterprise Virtualization:

- An unbeatable value combination of open source software on commodity x86 hardware
- An OpenStack distribution that enterprises can trust due to the certification of hardware vendors and ISVs, support, and stable and predictable releases with good lifecycles
- A large and growing open source community driving fast innovation into OpenStack

For the value proposition, we are building our OpenStack product as a completely open source offering, optimized for our RHEL-based KVM hypervisor on commodity x86 hardware. We are integrating OpenStack with the rest of our Open Hybrid Cloud portfolio, including CloudForms and OpenShift. We are in the process of hardening OpenStack into an enterprise-grade distribution, and this preview release is an important milestone in that process.

And is the ecosystem around OpenStack going to splinter like so many Unix variants? Or is it going to advance the pace of advancement in OpenStack? Time will tell. But, at Red Hat, as part of our Open Hybrid Cloud strategy, we are all in betting that OpenStack will advance. Unlike with Unix, the OpenStack community is all contributing to the same code base as part of the same structure—like Linux's community and unlike Unix's fiefdoms. The new OpenStack foundation is only going to help with that. And the OpenStack community is working together. It includes many of the same partners that we have around Linux. This is a group of companies that knows how to collaborate around an open source ecosystem.

OpenStack is going to advance, and we are betting it will win. The technology today is not yet where it needs to be. But neither was Linux when it took on Unix. The open source community—not the initial or current state of technology in 2002—is what propelled Linux to victory against proprietary Linux. And, open source versus proprietary is really the name of the game here.

Open source in a cloud world

The trend towards more permissive open source software licensing is not without controversy, especially given that it's commercial entities, rather than individual programmers, who often seem to be those most in favor of permissive licenses because of the fewer restrictions they impose. Permissive licenses, therefore, can be seen as part and parcel of open source commercialization—a trend some still view warily. Permissive licenses, such as BSD, Apache, and MIT, stemmed from decidedly non-commercial settings. But it's fair commentary that such licenses tend to be favored today for commercially-backed projects because of the flexibility they provide in packaging and embedding open source code in commercial offerings.

This controversy also directly dovetails into the intersection of open source and cloud computing.

For example, Bradley M. Kuhn, former executive director of the Free Software Foundation (FSF),[20] writes that: "Anyway, as you might suspect, I'm generally against the idea of relicensing from a copyleft to a non-copyleft license in most situations. In fact, I generally take the stance that you should go with the strictest copyleft possible unless there's a strong reason not to…. Frankly, if I were picking a license for OpenOffice.org and/or LibreOffice[21] [open source office productivity suites] from the start, I'd pick AGPLv3-or-later, because of the concern that it could be turned into a Google Docs-like web service."

The Affero GPL (AGPL) is a variant of the GPLv3 license intended to address the fact that the delivery of software in the form of a service, i.e. over the Web, doesn't count as distribution in most copyleft licenses—and therefore doesn't trigger the requirement that software

---

20. The Free Software Foundation was started by Richard Stallman; it advocates for free software ideals and works for adoption of free software and free media formats. The FSF also governs the GNU project, the core set of tools used by Linux, as well as the General Public License and its derivatives.

21. Variants on a popular open source office suite that includes a word processor.

changes be provided back to the community. Strong copyleft advocates view this as a loophole to be plugged with licenses like the AGPL; the AGPL, however, has not been widely adopted.

But the "cloud computing as loophole" school of thought rests on some of the same questionable assumptions as do arguments against permissive licenses in general.

The big implicit assumption is that, without adequate license protections, the entire communal development process will just wither away over time because corporations will simply take advantage of community work without giving back. A favorite proof point in favor of this argument is how Linux (which uses the copyleft GPL license) largely triumphed over BSD Unix (which predates Linux and was more capable early on, but which uses a far more permissive license that doesn't place any restrictions on proprietary extensions or use).

However, BSD has problems as an exemplar. Early BSD development was mired in all manner of fractious arguments between groups working with different "forks" of the code, as well as a prolonged legal battle with AT&T, which owned the Unix copyrights at the time. It is, therefore, an open historical question whether the GPL was the magic ingredient that led Linux to success or whether all manner of legal, community, and timing matters weren't ultimately much more important. In support of the contrary view, I'd note that, Linux aside, some of the most important open source projects—such as the Apache Webserver—do use BSD-like licenses. And, as we've seen, usage of permissive licenses is increasing.

Finally, extending the concept of distribution to cover Web services has practical problems. Distribution in the GPLv2 and GPLv3 licenses draws (mostly) a hard-edged line.[22] If you're an enterprise using software internally, anything goes. If you're using GPL code in

---

[22] "Mostly" because there are devilish details related to the exact manner in which code is linked together that still occasionally court controversy even twenty some years since the GPL was introduced.

software you're selling to the public–whether downloaded, on a CD, or in embedded firmware–you must make the relevant sources available. However, as more and more companies of every stripe make parts of their computing infrastructure available to their customers–think online banking, for example–the boundaries potentially become very fuzzy.

The bigger matter is that there are many other aspects of "freedom" in a cloud computing world, such as matters of privacy and data portability. For my part, I'd argue that open source has demonstrated that it can stand on its own without heroic measures to prop it up. Sure, continue to evangelize the benefits of open source and deal appropriately with those who don't follow license terms. But the more interesting, and important, questions lie elsewhere.

To focus on source code is to focus on a specific type of openness and freedom which was important historically. It's still highly relevant as a development model and remains an important enabler of other types of freedom.

But, in the case of Web services running on massive server farms and cooperating over a network with all manner of other code, services, and data, access to code has less value, less direct value anyway. After all, you could hardly just load up much of Google's software on a computer system and do anything useful with it. One needs the vast farms of server, interlocking pieces, and associated data. Also, the ability to view, modify, and redistribute source code is only one of many rights or protections to consider in a cloud computing world. For example, consider these other things that might matter more:

Ownership and portability of data. When you store information in a public cloud, can you get it back out? And can you get it back out in such a way that it's useful and portable? These questions become even more fraught when you consider that this is not a simple question of downloading files that you have stored on a disk somewhere on the network. Your "data" may also consist of your network and relationships to other data and people on a service such as Facebook. What type of portability even makes sense in that context?

Open APIs. Open source as we know it today evolved largely in the context of Unix-like operating systems and the programs that ran directly on top of them using "libc" and other system libraries.[23] While we may run monolithic programs over the network, much of the recent action on the Web has been in services such as Facebook, Flickr, Google Maps, and Salesforce.com which expose APIs at a higher level. This allows developers considerable freedom to extend these platforms. Thus, whether a platform or application is open source or not, given public and free-to-use APIs, it can be extended and consumed in ways somewhat analogous to open source. At the same time, the predictability and transparency of the terms of service for APIs—especially in the case of consumer-oriented services—raise their own issues.

Privacy and security. Eben Moglen of the Software Freedom Law Center once referred to Google and its ilk as a "private surveillance system that [the government] can subpoena at will." He went on to describe this as a "uniquely serious problem." It's hard to dispute that such services create an unprecedented centralization of data— both that data explicitly placed into the cloud and that generated with each search or purchase. This is anathema to those who saw open source and inexpensive computers as a great victory for the decentralization of computing and information.

From the perspective of maintaining user freedoms and choice, a key question of the cloud era will be translating the freedoms and advantages associated with open source to a new environment.[24] In the balance of this section, I'll explore this question in more detail.

---

[23] Open source came into being in an era when one wrote programs which ran on a specific operating system, such as one company's version of Unix. A later example would be programs written for Windows; typically, there is some but not absolute compatibility across versions of an operating system over time. This contrasts with newer Web-style languages that are typically fairly portable across operating systems.

[24] Of course, public cloud services, whether Facebook or less well-known examples, also raise new and complex issues such as how personally identifiable data can be correlated at massive scale. But these are beyond the scope of this book.

What makes a cloud open?

After one too many shouts punctuated by "In the name of the Queen!" by London's Master of Revels, Judi Dench's Queen Elizabeth in *Shakespeare in Love* rises to intone: "Mr Tilney! Have a care with my name - you will wear it out."

I sometimes feel similarly when it comes to the ferocity with which a lot of vendors apply the word "open" to cloud computing. Especially given that not a few of those involved aren't very open, after all. But they make up for the glancing and incidental ways their software and approaches are open with the volume of their rhetoric and the font size they use to display "OPEN" in their marketing literature.

But what does "open" mean in the context of building a hybrid cloud? It certainly doesn't begin and end with the submission of some format to a standards body or with an announcement of partners endorsing some specific technology platform. Nor is it just about open source. I don't claim that the following characteristics are definitive but they seem to leave a lot of IT professionals I meet with nodding their heads in agreement:

- **Is open source.** This allows adopters to control their particular implementation and doesn't restrict them to the technology and business roadmap of a specific vendor.

- **Has a viable, independent community.** Open source isn't just about the code, its license, and how it can be used and extended. At least as important is the community associated with the code and how it's governed.

- **Is based on open standards, or protocols and formats that are moving toward standardization, which are independent of their implementation.** Approaches to interoperability that aren't under the control of individual vendors and that aren't tied to specific platforms offer important flexibility.

- **Offers freedom to use intellectual property (IP).** Even "reasonable and non-discriminatory" license terms can still require permission or impose other restrictions on a technology's use.

- **Is deployable on the infrastructure of your choice.** Cloud management should not be tied to a specific virtualization or other foundational technology.

- **Is pluggable and extensible with an open API not under the control of a specific vendor or tied to a specific implementation.** This lets users add features, providers, and technologies from a variety of vendors or other sources.

- **Enables portability to other clouds.** Implicit in a cloud approach that provides support for heterogeneous infrastructure is that investments made in developing for an open cloud must be portable to other such clouds.

Of course, no one earns a perfect grade in every respect. Communities take time to develop. There are finite developer hours but an almost limitless variety of potentially supported infrastructure. And there will always be tradeoffs between value-add and perfect portability. However, I'd argue that, as a general rule, the more aspects in which a cloud is open, the greater value an organization can gain from that cloud.

Next, I take a look at each of these dimensions of openness in more detail.

Defining open for a hybrid cloud

Openness in cloud computing goes beyond open source, but open source is still important—especially to the degree that a hybrid cloud spans on-premise software in addition to hosted services.

Open source provides a degree of independence from the technology decisions and business practices of any single vendor. Even the best-intentioned vendors have to ultimately make choices about product roadmaps, pricing approaches, and target markets that may or may not align with the needs of a particular customer. Vendors get acquired, go out of business, and shift technology focus. That's life. And, with proprietary software, a customer ultimately doesn't have many options if a vendor isn't willing or able to provide support or, indeed, to continue selling the software at all. The only recourse may be to shift to another vendor, even if that means overhauling a large chunk of infrastructure. Open source reduces this lock-in.

This sort of flexibility is especially important in a cloud computing environment in which attaining the greatest value comes from spanning heterogeneous IT infrastructures. By cutting across silos of capacity, organizations can simplify their environments and thereby redirect people and capital from keeping the light on to driving innovation for their business.

Open source isn't just about preventing lock-in though. Open source puts users in control of their destiny and provides them with visibility into the technology on which they're basing their business. This is increasingly important as businesses are ever more driven by what technology makes possible from data analytics to mobile devices to real-time telemetry. Open source provides the headlights that give businesses an early view into what will be possible in the years ahead and therefore how best to position their business to take the greatest advantage of these coming possibilities.

But open source goes far beyond how individual organizations in isolation can leverage it. Open source also lets them collaborate with other communities and companies to help drive innovation in the areas that are important to them. This is an approach that is increasingly coming to the fore in this complex and connected world. Companies have seen how open source creates software that is not only a good value but that also often pushes forward the state of the art. Consequently, we see end-user organizations working cooperatively with each other and with vendors to drive innovations that are important to them in areas such as high performance communications and, yes, cloud.

Cloud computing started out, in many respects, as a user-driven phenomenon. "Shadow IT" use of consumer-oriented cloud services and public cloud providers set new expectations for IT departments. And with Linux and open source at the core of almost every major cloud provider, IT departments have no choice but to follow suit if they are to meet those expectations. With Linux and open source also prevalent throughout the Fortune 500 and other organizations worldwide, powering some of their largest and most mission-critical applications, it's logical to extend that open source to enterprise clouds as well.

But openness in a cloud requires more than just code that's under an open source license.

Historically, there's probably been too much attention paid to the details of open source licenses as opposed to the communities associated with bringing the code into being and using it. Certainly, licenses are important for defending against legal threats and in determining how an open source project can be combined with other projects. But without a viable, independent community, it's hard to realize the collaborative potential of open source. Delivering maximum innovation means having the right structures and organization in place to fully leverage the open source development model.

There's no single approach to fostering communities. The best approach in any given case to engaging with and governing a community will depend on the nature of the project. Who is contributing? What are the project's goals? What business or licensing constraints are there? These and many other factors will affect governance structure, as well as copyright, trademark, and licensing decisions.

It's also important for an open cloud to be based on open standards, or protocols and formats that are moving toward standardization. This is not a statement about needing to have "official" standards blessed by standards organizations. It's reasonable to expect that those will come about over time with various degrees of success and acceptance. But the history of formal technology standardization is one of trailing innovation, not leading it.

In the near term, other approaches to interoperability will likely be more important than standards as such. And the most effective interoperability mechanisms will be those that aren't under the control of individual vendors and that aren't tied to specific platforms, freeing protocols and formats from the constraints and limitations that come from being tied to a single vendor's business approach and product roadmap—even if those protocols or formats are nominally standards. The next chapter discusses this point in more detail.

An important side effect of this approach is that it allows specifications to evolve beyond implementation constraints. This creates the opportunity for communities and organizations to develop variants that meet their individual technical and commercial requirements. Perhaps one community values a feature-rich implementation, while another wants something that is simple—but lightning fast. If a specification for, say, a particular way of communicating between two systems is forced to be in lockstep with one specific implementation, only one set of tradeoffs are possible. Even if those tradeoffs are made out in the open as part of a process in which all stakeholders have a say, all parties still need to aim for a singular result. (Or, worse, the implementation ends up catering to so many parties that it ultimately doesn't satisfy anyone.)

If the specification and implementation are independent, on the other hand, there's a lot more flexibility to tailor code to the needs of different constituencies. It also enables and even encourages competing implementations, helping to push forward innovation. A good example of separating specification and implementation is the AMQP messaging protocol, an open standard for high performance messaging that was initially driven by end users in the financial industry. It has since become the *de facto* standard in that industry and is implemented in commercially-supported products such as Red Hat Enterprise Messaging and others.

Open clouds also have to give you the freedom to use intellectual property (IP). Permission to use intellectual property, like copyrights and patents, must be granted in ways that make the technology open and accessible to the user. So-called *"de facto* standards," which are often "standards" only insofar as they are promoted by a large vendor, can fail this test. Various open source licenses can provide certain types of protection against IP infringement claims, but freedom to use IP should still be regarded on its own, especially when using services or software for which no explicit grant or license has been given.

Other aspects of openness relate primarily to maintaining flexibility.

Cloud management is best not tied to a specific virtualization or other foundational technology. If all you can do with a cloud is to add a self-service front-end and some automation to a single vendor's proprietary virtualization product, you may have gained some efficiencies but you haven't extended the flexibility of a cloud to your broader IT infrastructure. That requires the ability to span physical servers, multiple virtualization platforms, and a wide range of public cloud providers. It requires being able to deploy to a choice of platforms on which to run applications, and to change that deployment decision as circumstances change.

Open APIs that are pluggable and extensible can help ensure deployment flexibility.

A pluggable and extensible architecture allows users to add features, providers, and technologies from a variety of vendors or other sources. Even an open API can be hard to extend and make use of if it's designed in a monolithic way that makes it difficult to add to incrementally—or that requires interfaces to be written using specific languages or frameworks.

It's best if the API isn't under the control of a specific vendor or tied to a specific implementation. Third-party foundations are one way that can allow for contributions and extensions in an open and transparent manner. As with other aspects of open source, it's not just about availability of source code, but the ability to truly take advantage of the innovation and community leverage which open source can deliver.

Implicit in a cloud approach that provides support for heterogeneous infrastructure is that investments made in developing for an open cloud should be portable to other such clouds. Portability takes a variety of forms, including computing services, programming languages and frameworks, data, and the applications themselves. Developing an application for one cloud shouldn't require a rewrite in a different language or with different APIs to move it elsewhere. Furthermore, a consistent runtime environment across clouds ensures that retesting and re-qualification isn't needed every time you want to redeploy.

Portability is closely tied to, and in many ways a product of, the other aspects of cloud openness. Without being able to deploy on a choice of infrastructure, you don't have portability. Without freedom from the business practices and technology roadmaps of individual vendors, you certainly won't have portability. Without open and extensible APIs, you can't have portability.

Portability requires thinking about how applications and data can be moved from one place to another and assessing the impact of such a move. Multiple technologies can come into play, although, ultimately, it's about making business decisions regarding the degree to which you're tied or not tied to a specific vendor or provider in some manner.

The ability to run workloads in a consistent way across a hybrid environment spanning both heterogeneous internal resources and public cloud providers is essential to effectively and efficiently taking advantage of cloud computing. Without this portability and choice, a cloud is a point solution that may deliver some local value but will not be transformational.

Of course, real world solutions will rarely, if ever, be perfectly open across all dimensions. Furthermore, users may choose to make tradeoffs between some vendor-specific functionality and a more open architecture. However, open source and all the aspects of openness that relate to it are increasingly just the reality of how software is developed and consumed.

Standard APIs: There's no substitute for open

Just because something is widely used doesn't make it a standard—*de facto*, *de jure*, or otherwise—in the sense that anyone can use and build implementations of that standard without restriction. Indeed, even standards that are "blessed" by powers-that-be are not always fully open in the ways that I have outlined previously.

Standardization has been around for a long time. The IEEE engineering professional organization tells us that:

> Based on relics found, standardization can be traced back to the ancient civilizations of Babylon and early Egypt. The earliest standards were the physical standards for weights and measures. As trade and commerce developed, written documents evolved that set mutually agreed upon standards for products and services, such as agriculture, ships, buildings and weapons. Initially, these standards were part of a single contract between supplier and purchaser. Later, the same standards came to be used across a range of transactions forming the basis for modern standardization.

A lot of this early standardization pretty much came down to custom. The convoluted history of why we drive on one side of the road in a given country is instructive. (Though each country's conventions are now enshrined in The Geneva Convention on Road Traffic.)

The history of the shipping container, recounted earlier, offers another, fairly typical, historical example. Incompatible container sizes and corner fittings required different equipment to load and unload and otherwise inhibited the development of a complete logistics system. The standardization that happened circa 1970 made possible the global shipping industry as we know it today—and all that implies. The evolution of standardized railroad gauges is similarly convoluted. The development of many early computer formats and protocols was equally Darwinian.

It's tempting to take this past as prologue and conclude that similar processes will continue to play out as computing moves forward and different forms of interoperability assume greater importance. For example, published application programming interfaces (API) are at the heart of how modular software communicates in a Web services-centric world. Software applications are increasingly composed of modular chunks of loosely coupled codes and data communication over the network, rather than monolithic single applications. One set of APIs wins and evolves. Another set of APIs becomes a favorite of some particular language community. Still another doesn't gain much traction and eventually withers and dies. It sounds like a familiar pattern.

But there's an important difference. In today's software world, it's impossible to ignore intellectual property matters whether copyright, patent, trademark, or otherwise. An API isn't a rail gauge—though perhaps today someone would try to patent that too.

As a result, tempting as it might be to adopt some API or other software construct because it's putatively a "*de facto*" standard (essentially a fancy, and somewhat loaded, way of saying it's popular)this adoption may not be such a good idea.

Stephen O'Grady, of analyst firm RedMonk, commented that:[25]

> it's worth noting that many large entities are already behaving as if APIs are in fact copyrightable. The most obvious indication of this is Amazon. Most large vendors we have spoken with consider Amazon's APIs a non-starter, given the legal uncertainties regarding the intellectual property involved. Vendors may in certain cases be willing to outsource that risk to a smaller third party – particularly one that's explicitly licensed like a Eucalyptus. But in general the low risk strategy for them has been to assume that Amazon would or could leverage their intellectual property rights – copyright or otherwise – around the APIs in question, and to avoid them as a result. Amazon, while having declined to assert itself directly on this basis, has also done nothing to discourage the perception that it has strict control of usage of its APIs. In doing so, it has effectively turned licensed access to the APIs into a negotiable asset, presumably an outcome that advocates of copyrightable APIs would like to see made common.

---

[25] http://redmonk.com/sogrady/2012/05/03/on-apis-copyright/

In fact, lack of openness can even extend to standards that have gained some degree of governmental or quasi-governmental approval—which is, after all, a political process. Last decade's fierce battle over Microsoft's submittal of its OOXML document format (used in recent versions of Microsoft Office) as a standard to the ECMA and ISO international standards organizations is perhaps the most visible example. The details of this particular fight are complicated, but, in Kurt Cagle's words, "The central crux of the [then-]current debate is, and should be, whether Microsoft's OOXML does in fact represent a standard that is conceivably implementable by anyone outside of Microsoft."

Issues of the conditions that should be satisfied in order for a vendor's preferred approach/format/etc. to become a "blessed" standard continue to reverberate. The latest round is about RAND (Reasonable-and-Non-Discriminatory) licensing and whether that can take the place of truly open implementations. It's essentially an attempt to slip proprietary approaches requiring a patent license into situations, such as government procurements, that require open standards.

But, as Simon Phipps, a Director of the Open Source Initiative and of the UK's Open Rights Group puts it:[26]

> The presence of RAND terms at best chills developer enthusiasm and at worst inhibits engagement, as for example it did in the case of Sender ID at IETF. As Välimäki and Oksanen say, RAND policy allows patent holders to decide whether they want to discourage the use of open source. Leaving that capability in the hands of some (usually well-resourced) suppliers seems unwise.

At one level, the takeaway here might be "it's complicated." And it is. But another takeaway is pretty simple. You can dress up proprietary standards in various ways and with various terms and such standards have a place, even an important one, in the IT ecosystem. But they're not open, whatever you call them.

---

[26] http://blogs.computerworlduk.com/simon-says/2012/04/open-standards-consultation-guide/index.htm See also http://www.law.ed.ac.uk/ahrc/script-ed/vol2-3/valimaki.asp

The freedom to leave by Simon Phipps

Simon Phipps is an independent consultant providing insight and knowledge on open source to businesses and governments worldwide. He is also President of the Open Source Initiative, the non-profit organization that advocates for open source software and builds bridges between open source communities and maintains the canonical list of open source licenses. His writing is featured in InfoWorld, ComputerWorld, O'Reilly Radar and other publications. He is a Director of the UK's Open Rights Group as well as on the advisory board of Open Source for America.

Adapted from a post originally posted Jun 27 2006.

Website: http://webmink.com/

Twitter: @webmink

A journalist asked me an interesting question once. "Why is it," he asked, "that we are seeing so many new online and desktop tools at the moment?" There's loads of energy around, with projects like Google Calendar, KOffice, OpenOffice.org and plenty more, plus new innovations of many kinds. I've tried many of these and some of them have stuck. What's the connection between them?

The New Lock-Out

The thing is, all of these tools have worked out that lock-in is the new lock-out. The fastest way to send early adopters packing is to make your cool new toy a roach motel. To start with, early adopters like me are not willing to put live data into applications that don't offer import and export. My calendar is in RFC2445 iCalendar format, so if you want me to try your new calendar thing you'd better accept that as the import format. If I can't add iCalendar and vCalendar appointments I'll not be using it for long, and there had better be an iCalendar sharing facility for scheduling.

What's more, I have to have iCalendar export so I can migrate away from your new toy to things like Apple iCal, Google Calendar or any of the umpteen programs that support those standards. The same goes for everything else – I just moved my blog subscriptions from one tool to another I wanted to try using OPML export, and I work with a group of people routinely exchanging documents between a selection of applications that support ODF.

Confidence To Stay

The availability of open, freely-usable standards creates a bigger market and promotes innovation because we are all free to give things a try, as was clear at BloggerCon. If "interoperability" meant "import only", I'd never feel safe trying new things so market growth and innovation would be inhibited. People who implement open standards like this are smart, because although they allow customers to leave for greener pastures they also allow them to return – I am still using Bloglines despite the appeal of the new tool – and the confidence I feel over "owning" my data makes me a much more interesting customer.

That feeling is caused by more than interoperability – it takes full substitutability for me to have the confidence to stay as well as the freedom to leave. That's why Stewart was spot-on with Flickr's policy and paradoxically kept my business by allowing me to leave at any time.[27]

Innovation Enabled

More than that, though, full support for truly open standards means that new ways to use the data can occur. For example, the feeds in

---

[27] Steward Butterfield, the co-founder of Flickr, promised that the service would allow any of its commercial competitors the API access needed to help customers switch away from Flickr to a competing service; the only gotcha was that these competitors needed to offer the same deal to Flickr to help their customers switch, too.

Bloglines mean I can use a feed reader to read the for:webmink tag feed and have [Michael] Coté send me interesting links to read without the overhead of e-mail. That's part innovation-by-design and part innovation-enabled, leaving the customer to work out new ways to mash-up the data and create innovative uses for their own data. When using the data demands only a particular vendor's software, or a licensing relationship, or some other boundary traversal, the innovation finds it harder to escape.

So what does it take to have a standard that leads to substitutability and the freedom to leave? At a minimum, it takes the following to innovation-enable a standard.

- First of all, it takes confidence over intellectual property rights. I dream of a world where "standard" implies that all parties to the creation of the specification have been compelled to issue non-assert covenants so every developer can be sure there's no strings attached.

- Second, it takes multiple implementations, proving the format is actually usable in multiple places. This was the genius of IETF and it's one of the lessons of CORBA.

- Third, the approach must not favour any particular implementation or platform. That's the problem Microsoft's Office 12 XML format (or whatever it's called today) turns out to have, and no amount of rubber-stamping by the vendor-only Ecma International will fix it.

- Fourth, and in the coming world of development the most important, is that there's an open source reference implementation, so that the standard can be incorporated into as many systems as possible. This, by the way, is why I am such a fan of open source for the Java platform.

The Richness of the Plains

This is about far more than interoperability. Interoperability was a fine goal in the 90s, but in today's world it takes much more than just the minimum level of allowing others to use your secret sauce. Pragmatic interoperability is better than nothing and sure beats the cold-war mindset of the 80s and 90s where incompatibility and isolationism were the rule. But I want more than import-only. I want more than lowest-common-denominator exchange, where I have to rework my data to make it survive the teleport. Those are the hallmarks of the monopolist's definition of interoperability – letting you play in my market at little risk to me.

The network changes everything. I argue in my current keynote that injecting the network into society removes the commercial benefits previously achieved by closed behaviour, and the plethora of new software the journalist observed seems to support that. The canyons were the first world of software and interoperability was their high-altitude pass. The plains are the new world, where the spread of open formats and software grows the market and gives us all the opportunity for success – in whatever compatible way we choose to measure it.

The new world is being made by iCalendar, Atom/RSS, OpenDocument, OPML and their like, overturning one of Robert X. Cringeley's five lock-ins[28] in a world that's also rejecting the other four. Truly open formats are creating the new market, and those who attempt to subvert the trend with pseudo-openness will fail.

---

[28]   1. Announce a direction, not a product (people will put off buying competing products because you've just told them they're the old way of doing things).

2. Announce a real product, but do so long before you actually expect to deliver, disrupting the market for competing products that are already shipping.

3. Don't announce a product, but do leak a few strategic hints, even if they aren't true.

4. Don't support anybody else's standards; make your own.

5. Announce a product, then say you don't really mean it.

Building Hybrid Clouds

The public cloud has set a new benchmark for IT departments. But that doesn't mean that everything can just move into a public cloud. For in-house modernization, virtualization is a good starting point, but that's not the complete answer either. For one thing, virtualization (by itself) mostly just focuses on improving the efficiency and utilization of servers; it doesn't really address new ways of thinking about the way applications interact and are delivered to users.

Organizations are increasingly looking to span hybrid infrastructure whether that means heterogeneous in-house resources or a combination of in-house and public IT of various types. And they're looking to evolve to new ways of thinking about IT services.

A new benchmark for IT departments

As we've seen, when the term cloud computing first appeared on the scene, it described a public computing utility. A clear historical analogue was electricity: Generated by large service providers. Delivered over a grid. Paid for when it's consumed and by the amount used.

A public cloud built around this utility premise can be compelling when compared to traditional enterprise IT. The cost per unit of computing can be much lower than was the historical norm for an IT department to buy a server and manage it. Users, such as developers, can use a credit card to get access to IT resources in minutes, rather than waiting months for a new server to be approved, requisitioned, and provisioned. And improvements to cloud technology's efficiency and agility can help bring new applications and business services (and their associated revenue streams) online more quickly.

In short, public cloud providers such as Amazon Web Services have set a new benchmark for internal IT departments. These expectations are further fueled by the experiences all of us have as consumers. We expect applications to be attractive and interactive, accessible from all of our devices anytime and anywhere, and with new features and capabilities added on Internet time, not enterprise software time.

However, most organizations are not ready to move all of their applications onto public cloud providers. They often have concerns around compliance and governance, especially for mission-critical production applications or those that touch sensitive customer data. (Even if those concerns aren't always well-founded, they nonetheless exist.) And public clouds can't usually be customized and optimized for unique business needs.

Because so many organizations—especially large ones—aren't prepared to go all-in with public clouds, there is great interest in building hybrid clouds that span on-premise and off-premise resources to deliver the best of both worlds: public cloud economics and agility optimized for private enterprise needs such as audit, risk management, and strong policy management.

Numerous IT industry analysts estimate that about 70 to 80 percent of the money spent in a typical IT organization goes into routine processes and updates, keeping the lights on so to speak, and only the small balance is genuinely focused on innovations moving the business forward. One of the great hopes of cloud computing, with its emphasis on automation, flexibility, and self-service, is that these numbers can be flipped. A redirection of resources from keeping the lights on to innovation could have a big effect in a world in which more and more businesses are enabled by what they can accomplish using information.

As a result, choosing how to approach cloud computing is a big strategic decision facing many organizations today. Ultimately the decision will affect their competitiveness, flexibility, and IT economics. For many, that decision will involve building a hybrid cloud that bridges public clouds with in-house private clouds.

There are a variety of approaches to building such a a hybrid cloud. However, among the most important considerations are:

- An architecture that avoids creating new IT silos

- An approach to openness that goes beyond just open source

- The ability to manage distributed applications running across the hybrid infrastructure

In short, the transition to cloud computing remains as important as its early proponents said it would be. But it's not playing out like they thought: it's about hybrid clouds, not just compute utilities.

Cloud computing's big surprise

Something funny happened on the way to the cloud. Many applications, especially those used by consumers and smaller businesses, did indeed shift to public cloud providers like Google. However, with some exceptions, the trend in large organizations is something quite different. The idea of there being a "Big Switch" in the sense of all computing shifting to a handful of mega-service providers has been overstated, at least for practically interesting time horizons.

In part, this is because computing introduces complications that the electric utility lacks.[29] The electrons powering a motor don't have privacy and security considerations. The electrons encoding a Social Security number in a data center do. Plenty of other technical and governance concerns also conspire to make computing less utility-like. Computing never was and never will be as simple and standardized as what comes out of a wall socket.

Moreover, as Andi Mann—formerly a fellow analyst and now with software management giant CA—notes, even the cost benefits of public clouds aren't necessarily a given:[30]

> Public cloud can be cheaper than on-premise IT or private cloud, especially for selected services and SMBs [small and medium businesses]. However for large enterprises, while there are plenty of reasons to use public cloud, cost reduction is not always one of them.

> Public cloud certainly has a low start-up cost, but also a long ongoing cost. For all practical purposes, the ongoing cost is never-ending too. As long as you need it, you keep paying as much as you did on day one, without adding an asset to your books or depreciating your facilities investments.

---

[29] To be sure, there are plenty of complications in the infrastructure required to generate and deliver the electric utility but most of this is rarely, if ever, exposed to the consumer of the service.

[30] http://pleasediscuss.com/andimann/20110504/the-cost-benefit-myth-of-the-public-cloud/

One report from management consultants McKinsey even provided some hard data suggesting that public clouds actually cost more. The report was somewhat controversial at the time and critiques flew around online. But whatever the specifics of a given case, the reality is that when I speak with CIOs at large enterprises, I don't think I've heard one argue that public cloud resources can universally reduce costs. And this isn't a matter of reflexive "server hugging." There is equal unanimity that using shared resources for certain workloads and use cases does save money and bring other benefits.

The key to economically running many or most IT services internally seems to be finding a level of scale at which, to use a term from retired IBMer Irving Wladawsky-Berger, data center operations can be "industrialized" — which is to say standardized, made process-driven, and highly automated; at a scale, in other words, in which operational processes associated with large public cloud providers can be implemented in a dedicated way for a single organization.

From the perspective of a company which owns and operates its own facilities, this point is probably somewhere around one or two data centers (given the need for some spare capacity for redundancy), although using co-location providers[31] and other ways of obtaining dedicated capacity within a shared physical infrastructure may drive necessary scale points even lower. And these economic realities are reflected in the forecasts of IT analyst firms like Forrester and IDC, all of which see rapid growth in private clouds.

And it's this widespread interest in building private clouds that's been one of the big surprises of cloud computing's still early years. The cloud discussion began as a shift to a fundamentally different economic model under which even large organizations would rent computing rather than building and owning it. Some of that's happening, but it's turning out to be just part of the cloud computing storyline.

---

[31] With "colo," you own and operate your own servers in most respects, but the physical infrastructure, such as power and cooling, is provided by someone else.

Indeed, for organizations that view IT as a strategic asset—and more and more do—cloud computing is often less about adopting public clouds for their low costs and more about adopting their processes and applying them to the private cloud. In this case, cloud computing is far more about helping the business increase revenues than cutting the total cost of IT.

This tension between private and public utilities—and indeed between decentralized and centralized computing—will doubtless continue to play out, as indeed it has for decades, in various ways. Many utility concepts remain in play and offer powerful insights. Self-service, the ability to quickly grow up and shrink down, and even a degree of standardization are leading to fundamentally better ways of approaching information technology in many organizations. But, for the planning horizon relevant to most people working in IT—say, five to ten years tops—the realities should be pretty clear. They are going to use a mix of private and public computing. They're going to be hybrid.[32]

---

[32] The details will depend on the organization. Smaller companies of the sort that have no real IT staff today will tend to flock to public clouds fairly quickly, especially in the form of Software-as-a-Service applications that typically don't require a lot of expertise to use. And certain startups will at least start out without buying their own servers, although there are examples, such as the Netflix video rental service and the SmugMug online photo-sharing and storage business, that have famously continued to use Amazon Web Services almost exclusively even as they've grown to be sizable businesses.

Whence Virtualization

This is a book about cloud, not about virtualization. Cloud computing is about more than virtualization and is, at least in principle, independent of it. "Bare metal," which is to say computer systems just running an operating system like Linux or Microsoft Windows can be part of clouds as well. But the reality is that virtualization is intimately tied to cloud computing in a lot of ways.

This makes virtualization worth discussing. But it's also worth considering what virtualization actually is and what problems it was invented to solve, and how it differs from cloud in many respects.

For much of the first decade of the 21st century, inspired by both hype and legitimate customer excitement, many vendors took to using the "virtualization" moniker more as the hip phrase of the moment than as something that's supposed to convey any actual meaning. (A bit like cloud computing, truth be told.)

It didn't help matters that virtualization, in the broad sense of "remapping physical resources to more useful logical ones," spans a huge swath of technologies. Indeed, the concept of abstraction is pervasive throughout computing. However, one particular set of related approaches turned out to help solve a very specific and costly problem. Server virtualization let you use a physical server that you had purchased much more efficiently, by letting you run more programs side by side with each other. But we're getting ahead of ourselves.

The idea behind server virtualization is actually quite an old one. What we call virtualization today was intimately intertwined with early developments in time-shared computing that took place in Cambridge, Massachusetts during the early Sixties—where the Compatible Time-Sharing System (CTSS), running on a multi-million dollar IBM 7094, was developed at MIT. But GE won out for the competition to succeed CTSS;[33] MIT saw GE as more committed to time-sharing than IBM, which they saw as generally holding an opposing batch-processing view of the world.[34] There was doubtless much truth to that characterization, which flavored the second-class-citizen aspect of virtual machine technology at IBM for many years.

IBM's early work didn't go away. Part of IBM's project involved CP-67, a program that made one physical computer look like several virtual ones. It let the virtual machines share processor cycles and memory and it divided the physical disk into small virtual disks. You could run the same operating system on the physical machine and a virtual one. You could also run CMS, which was expressly-designed as a single-user system to take advantage of CP-67 multiprogramming so that many users could run on the same hardware independently of each other.

Virtualization remained largely in the background at IBM. But fast forward 25 years and Linux was starting to make headlines as part of the first Internet build-out. IBM made the promotion of Linux a crucial part of its corporate strategy. As part of this effort, it also dusted off its virtualization technology—by then called z/VM. Running Linux on its expensive in-house developed "Big Iron" mainframe servers only made sense if you could share that hardware, which could cost upwards of $1 million a box, across a very large number of Linux copies. And doing that required virtual machines.

VMs are software abstractions, a way to fool operating systems and their applications into thinking that they have access to a real (i.e. physical) server when, in fact, they have access to only a subset of one. Each VM then has its own independent "guest" OS and applications

---

[33] The overall competition was for Project MAC, which included MULTICS, the replacement to CTSS. MULTICS was a commercial failure but it helped birth a wide range of concepts that went on to define how operating systems would be built.

[34] The stereotypical, but not inaccurate, view of batch computing at the time was that you submitted a "deck" of punch cards to be processed and came back hours later for the results printed out on wide pin-fed paper. With time-sharing, multiple users were given the appearance of being able to use a single system at the same time.

are not even aware of any other VMs that may be running on the same box, other than through the system's usual network interactions with other systems. Thus, the operating systems and applications within VMs are isolated from each other in much the same manner as if they were running on separate physical servers. They're created by a special piece of software called a virtual machine monitor (VMM), often called a "hypervisor," that sits on top of the hardware, where it creates and manages one or more VMs sitting on top. The hypervisor abstracts away the physical server and essentially presents a sort of doppelgänger of that server to any software running on the machine.

Linux on mainframe virtual machines became a hugely successful initiative for IBM. By the end of 2006, IBM was reporting that more than 60 percent of its mainframe revenue came from "new" workloads, and that about 20 percent of revenue and 30 percent of "MIPS" (i.e. computing cycles) were coming from Linux customers.

But, in the meantime, virtualization came to the mainstream market running x86 servers, an event with ultimately broader implications.

In 1998, a company called VMware was founded in Palo Alto, California by Diane Greene, her husband Mendel Rosenblum, Scott Devine, Edward Wang, and Edouard Bugnion. Initially, the company focused on the needs of software developers. It did so by giving them a product that let them create multiple "virtual machines" (VMs) hosted atop a single copy of a standard operating system such as Windows or Linux. This allowed each developer to have multiple operating system copies on his workstation. This let the developers recover from failures faster and aided in testing against multiple software versions on a single workstation.

However, over time, virtualization on mainstream x86 servers evolved in directions that made it more suitable for running more performance-sensitive workloads on back-end servers—an evolution of technology that coincided with the bursting of the dot-com bubble in about 2001.

It turned out that server virtualization and a crashing IT market made for a serendipitous pairing. Typical mass-market servers were woefully underutilized. According to most measures, only 15 percent or so of their capacity was being used to do work. The reason was that x86 servers and operating systems, having evolved from the PC, had mostly been designed with a view towards supporting single users running single applications. As a result, especially on servers running the Microsoft Windows operating system, it was difficult to run multiple applications side-by-side without them interfering with each other. The isolation provided by VMs provided a relatively easy and cost-effective fix.[35]

Server virtualization essentially provided free capacity—well, free except for the considerable revenues that VMware began to rake in. It was a compelling story for a cash-starved time; server virtualization took off like a rocket.

VMware itself was purchased by EMC, a large storage vendor; in retrospect, it was one of the better acquisition deals of the 2000s. At the same time, as in the case of operating systems like Linux, open source began to make strides in virtualization in the latter part of the decade. In parallel, microprocessor vendors Intel and AMD designed in features that made the x86 architecture easier to virtualize with less overhead; unlike IBM mainframes, x86 had never been designed with virtualization in mind.

A project called Xen, out of the University of Cambridge, was the first to make a major mark in open source virtualization. However, in 2006, the KVM (Kernel-based Virtual Machine) project emerged from Qumranet, a startup based in Santa Clara, California, with research and development in Israel. Its CTO was Moshe Bar, who had co-founded XenSource, the commercial entity behind the Xen project.

As CNET reporter Stephen Shankland noted in a February 2007 story:

---

[35] The situation with Linux, by then emerging as the other mainstream x86 operating system, wasn't so dire because Linux was an open source variant of the Unix family of operating systems, which had long embraced multi-user and multi-program environments.

Unlike Xen additions to Linux, the KVM patch slipped nearly instantly into the mainstream kernel maintained by Torvalds and a group of deputies.

"We did things the Linux way," [Qumranet employee Avi] Kivity said in an interview. "I am a longtime lurker on the Linux kernel mailing list, so I know what's important to the kernel maintainers and tried to get things right the first time. Where I got things wrong, I fixed them quickly."

He introduced KVM with source code, not words. "Kernel maintainers only take you seriously if the first word in a message is 'PATCH,'" Kivity said.

Torvalds, who accepted the first KVM patches in December, said the technology's lack of intrusiveness and complications led to its inclusion.

"One reason KVM was so easy to merge was that it was really fairly straightforward, from the kernel's point of view," Torvalds said. And KVM programmers were easier to deal with than Xen programmers, he added: "I think they just had a lot less politics, and very few general policy issues."

In short, while Xen remained a separate entity that had to be carefully paired with the Linux kernel whenever it was updated, KVM was incorporated directly, which, among other advantages, lets it benefit from performance and security work done for Linux. For these and other reasons, Red Hat bought Qumranet in 2008 for $107 million.

Since that time KVM has gained significant attention. A marketing partnership, the Open Virtualization Alliance, was formed in May of 2011 to promote KVM and had over 200 members as of March 2012. Associated virtualization management open source work was formalized into the oVirt project later that year.

Today, virtualization remains just one way to control the applications running on a physical server. And that's what virtualization is, really, a type of workload management.

Especially in large cloud environments with more specialized needs, the various isolation and optimization tools that work within a single copy of an operating system can be a more efficient foundation for cloud computing than virtual machines. VMs have associated overhead because they bring along all the code associated with an operating system for each "guest" VM and its associated applications. Operating systems make convenient guest containers for a variety of reasons, but they're not particularly lightweight.

However, for mainstream enterprise customers and for Infrastructure-as-a-Service public clouds, which are largely in the business of offering pay-as-you-go VMs, server virtualization is an important component of a cloud architecture.

Virtualization as cloud foundation

So far, we've seen how virtualization allows multiple workloads to be consolidated onto a single physical server—thereby increasing server utilization and lowering costs. But that is really a side effect of how a hypervisor inserts an abstraction layer between the server hardware and any software sitting on top.

This abstraction breaks the bonds between applications and specific physical servers and simplifies moving applications from one physical location to another. Or, more accurately, it simplifies moving the aggregation of operating system, application or applications, and supporting software bits known as a virtual machine.

The simplification comes about because, when software is installed directly on hardware, it's not always easy to pick it up and move it elsewhere. It's bound to a particular piece of hardware, in a sense. The stickiness comes about because software, when it's installed, often adapts itself to the specifics of the underlying server. For instance, it might install code that is unique to a particular networking chip model. Rip out that image and plop it down on another server with different hardware and things may not work properly.

By contrast, a virtualization layer abstracts away many of these server specifics, presenting software with idealized abstractions that paper over many of the hardware details. It's therefore much easier to move images sitting on top of this abstraction layer than images sitting directly on the underlying hardware. (Essentially, the hypervisor takes over from the layers of an operating system tasked to interface with the server hardware.)

In practice, moving workloads from one physical server to another isn't as dire as I've painted it. x86 server hardware is standardized in many respects and operating systems are increasingly capable of dynamically dealing with live changes to the systems on which they run. These are among the reasons that cloud computing doesn't always require a virtualized foundation. Nonetheless, virtualization's characteristics fit well with a cloud environment in which services, such as applications, run at a level of abstraction divorced from server details.

Indeed, one way of thinking of a cloud is as an additional level of resource abstraction sitting above virtualization. Virtualization carves up physical servers in virtual chunks of compute capacity, networking links, and storage. A cloud then builds a resource pool from these virtual abstractions and deploys workloads into those pools based on policy.

Dealing with scale and computing complexity, as virtualization and cloud computing both do, by adding layers of abstraction isn't a new idea in computing. In fact, the history of computing technology is essentially a history of layering abstraction upon abstraction. Each layer tithes a bit of the additional capacity and performance provided by new technology and, in exchange, it autonomously deals with underlying complexity. File systems, high-level programming languages, virtual memory, and many features of an operating system are all examples of abstractions. Without these abstractions, we'd never to be able to tap the power of modern computer systems because we'd be spending so much time dealing with the myriad low-level housekeeping tasks . Computers are nothing if not literal.

The anatomy of a hybrid cloud

Before getting into how one might go about building a hybrid cloud, let's take a look at what a hybrid cloud looks like architecturally. For purposes of illustration, I'm going to use Red Hat's current portfolio as of early 2013 as an illustration, but you'd see certain common aspects in the products and product lines of other vendors.

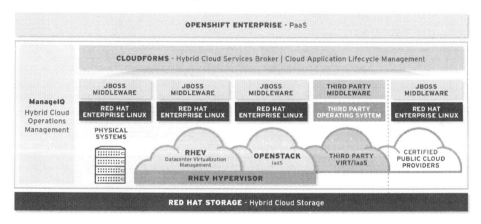

Virtualization and Infrastructure-as-a-Service

At the bottom is the infrastructure layer. This typically consists of a hypervisor, its associated infrastructure management stack, and APIs that provide the ability to control that management stack through programmatic means. APIs are the mechanism by which different software programs, such as the different layers of a software stack, communicate with each other.

This layer includes virtualization. A hybrid cloud can include multiple flavors of virtualization. In Red Hat's case, virtualization is provided by the KVM hypervisor and the associated management found in Red Hat Enterprise Virtualization (RHEV). The associated upstream community project for this virtualization management is called oVirt. RHEV provides virtualization management for an "enterprise use case." It supports hardware such as Storage Area Networks[36] and features such as the Live Migration of running instances from one server to another that are valued in traditionally-architected IT shops.

One can think of an Infrastructure-as-a-Service like OpenStack as virtualization management evolving to "cloud use cases" that consist of more distributed server and software architectures and an emphasis on user self-service.

Perhaps the easier way to think of OpenStack, however, is that it lets an IT organization stand up a cloud that looks and acts like a cloud at a service provider. Thus, in addition to letting a user request an image (a virtual machine, really) through self-service, OpenStack also offers storage and other services of types that would be familiar to users of a public cloud service.

That OpenStack is focused on this public cloud-like use case shouldn't be surprising; service provider Rackspace has been an important contributor to OpenStack and uses code from the project for its own public cloud offering.

Over time, we should expect to see virtualization management converge into products that can handle a range of use cases, rather than falling into distinct "enterprise" and "cloud" worlds as they generally do today. This is a natural progression as the distinctions between enterprise-style applications and cloud-style-applications crumble. Or, indeed, as cloud-style becomes the way that more and more applications are built.

Public IaaS clouds

Alternatively, the self-service infrastructure may be at a public cloud provider such as Amazon Web Services or Rackspace. Ultimately their goal is to make the underlying infrastructure decisions largely

---

[36] SANs lets multiple physical servers share relatively expensive disk arrays which include sophisticated hardware to provide data protection and other features. They're commonly associated with traditional enterprise data centers and database systems which require redundancy and data integrity at the hardware level.

transparent to the consumer of the resources, such as a developer. Of course, where the resources are located, how they are managed, and what types of hardware functions they expose make a big different to the ops team. But they're deliberately abstracted from those developing and using applications. Public clouds, as we've seen, are also interesting to many organizations as they enable paying for capacity only as it's consumed and they let organizations delegate the purchase and operations of computing hardware to others.

Physical servers

Even when virtualization and cloud computing aren't being conflated, we often see virtualization promoted as a prerequisite for cloud computing. It isn't.

To be sure, the most familiar examples of clouds which don't use virtualization to any significant degree are online giants such as Google Applications and Facebook. But they're delivering software services of various types, not raw computing infrastructure or even a platform for developers. They're also very large scale and relatively homogeneous. These characteristics make it easier for them to use a somewhat more efficient non-virtualized infrastructure under the covers.

However, there is also a subset of on-premise servers that won't necessarily be virtualized. Red Hat ran a survey at VMworld, VMware's user show, in 2011. We asked "What percentage of applications do you plan to virtualize?" Almost half planned to virtualize 75 percent of their application infrastructure with almost another quarter planning to virtualize 50 percent. However, it's worth noting that only 17 percent planned to virtualize everything. This is consistent with the results seen by various industry analysts.

Hybrid cloud management

These different types of infrastructure can be thought of as "cloud providers." In Red Hat's case, CloudForms is the hybrid cloud management product that cuts across disparate cloud provider resources. It lets you build and manage a "cloud of clouds" in a sense.

To break things down a bit, it's useful to think of hybrid cloud management as including a hybrid cloud broker, cloud application lifecycle management, and hybrid cloud operations management.

A hybrid cloud broker can be thought of as the piece that allows you to build a hybrid cloud in the first place. It unifies, not only private and public cloud services, but also heterogeneous on-premise infrastructure—such as multiple virtualization platforms. The hybrid cloud broker isn't itself virtualization or Infrastructure-as-a-Service infrastructure, but it enables the construction of a hybrid cloud from a pool of resources spanning a diverse set of infrastructure that may use varied APIs and image formats.

One function of a hybrid cloud broker is to act as a sort of translation shim across heterogeneous virtualization and cloud platforms. Different clouds use different application programming interfaces (APIs) even for similar tasks, such as loading a file into an object store. They require that uploaded images (typically an operating system and an associated workload) be in a specific format related to the underlying virtualization platform used by the cloud provider. The hybrid cloud broker needs to manage these differences, while retaining the ability to leverage as much of a given provider's unique functionality as possible. In the case of CloudForms, the Apache Deltacloud Project is the technology which lets workloads be deployed across a hybrid mix of cloud providers.

The hybrid cloud broker is also responsible for the placement of workloads, subject to any policies system administrators have embedded in a workload. For example, policy may require that an application processing confidential customer data only be deployed on private infrastructure. Over time, hybrid cloud brokers have the potential to evolve capabilities such as dynamically allocating workloads based on the spot market cost of various types of infrastructure. However, today, it's more realistic (in terms of both the technology and the interests of most users) to think of hybrid cloud brokers as enabling the use of heterogeneous infrastructure and workload migration, but migration that's generally manual and takes place over relatively long time horizons rather than automated and minute-by-minute.

The second area of hybrid cloud management is application lifecycle management: building and managing applications within a hybrid cloud. This allows IT departments to offer the agility and benefits of self-service access to cloud resources while still retaining control of workloads, wherever they're running.

One of the mechanisms enabling policy-based self-service in hybrid cloud environments is templates, called Application Blueprints in the case of CloudForms. A template defines the software components— and configuration details about the application and the target environment; this allows the application to be run on a wide variety of infrastructure types, subject to any restrictions that system administrators may impose.

Application lifecycle management also involves managing the compliance and governance of running applications against their template.. This includes the ability to patch, configure, perform drift detection, apply security errata, and manage licenses or subscriptions.

It's worth noting that application lifecycle management takes place at the level of the application, not the operating system container— which is to say the virtual machine in the case of virtualized infrastructure—that holds the application. In this respect, application lifecycle management is different from basic virtualization management, which is more concerned with managing VMs than their associated content.

The final area of hybrid cloud management is hybrid cloud operations management tools including monitoring, management, and automation across virtual and cloud infrastructure through a unified interface. This includes tools used to discover, automate, monitor, measure and govern virtualization and cloud infrastructures. At a higher level, operations management is about service lifecycle management that provides provisioning, intelligent workload management, metering, cost transparency, and the retirement of resources when they are no longer required. ManageIQ, a late 2012 Red Hat acquisition, adds orchestration capabilities such as chargeback that will be folded into CloudForms.

Platform-as-a-Service

So far, this discussion has been infrastructure-centric although many principles apply across cloud computing more broadly. By infrastructure-centric I mean that the resources which users are exposed to are at the level of a provisioned operating system instance (a virtual machine). In other words, the user sees an IaaS cloud as a particularly fast and easy way to get a new server delivered, but not necessarily something different in kind.

Such familiarity isn't necessarily bad. However, Platform-as-a-Service (PaaS) offers a different level of abstraction that is more focused on the typical concerns of developers and those supporting them.[37] Thus, instead of an operating system image-centric view, PaaS is more oriented to a view that revolves around pushing and pulling code into and out of repositories; the operation of the software needed to run that code is largely kept in the background.

Unlike a PaaS that is limited to a specific provider, Red Hat's OpenShift PaaS can run on top of any appropriately provisioned infrastructure whether in a hosted or on-premise environment. It then provides application multi-tenancy within the operating system images that make up the infrastructure. It does so using a combination of SELinux for security isolation, Cgroups for resource control, and other Linux features.

This approach allows organizations to not only use the languages and frameworks of their choice but also to select the IT operational model most appropriate to their needs. The provisioning and ongoing management of the underlying infrastructure on which OpenShift PaaS runs is where virtualization, IaaS, and cloud management

---

[37] Like many things associated with cloud computing, PaaS too can refer to a some only vaguely related things. Our discussion here focuses on PaaS as a general purpose cloud abstraction for developers.

solutions come in. PaaS will be discussed in more detail later in the book.

What of cloudbursting?

Talk of hybrid clouds often leads to talk of "cloudbursting," the idea that there can be some automagical movement of applications from place to place based on relative pricing or other ephemeral factors.

Such talk makes people like Chris Hoff "want to punch kittens."[38] As he put it in one blog post: "It's used by people to describe a use case in which workloads that run first and foremost within the walled gardens of an enterprise, magically burst forth into public cloud based upon a lack of capacity internally and a plethora of available capacity externally."

More colorful language followed in this particular broadside. But the gist was that, if an application passes the hurdles of being able to run in a public cloud—regulatory compliance, acceptable performance, legal implications, and so forth—then why wouldn't you just run the application in a public cloud, period? After all, there's a sort of default assumption that public clouds like Amazon are cheaper than in-house IT. The only wrinkle is that they won't always meet your IT governance requirements.

Put another way, private and public clouds have different operational models and it's unclear why you'd want to mix them.

But cloudbursting, as the term is typically used, is something of a red herring.

The economics of running data centers are such that a large public cloud provider can't necessarily operate modern, standardized, well-managed data centers for markedly lower costs than does Fortune 100 Megacorp. Does Megacorp have more operational complexities and associated costs? Probably. But that's also sort of beside the point. Unless a given workload can run on a standardized infrastructure, it can't run on an external cloud provider anyway.

---

[38] http://www.rationalsurvivability.com/blog/2011/04/incomplete-thought-cloudbursting-your-bubble-i-call-bullshit/ Hoff currently works for Juniper Networks.

Still, if internally hosted capacity, especially excess capacity, can indeed be cheaper (at least in terms of marginal costs) than a public cloud, then cloudbursting may still make economic sense for certain applications. Put another way, it may be cheaper to use internal capacity first, but it may not be cheaper to build enough internal capacity to handle all spikes in demand.

That said, I agree with Hoff's basic point.

Spot markets for computing capacity have long hovered around the horizon—a recent example was Enomaly's SpotCloud prior to its acquisition by Virtustream. However, as was the case during the spike of interest in peer-to-peer computing about ten years ago (think SETI@Home), the hurdles to mainstream adoption are considerable. Standards for interoperability are just the beginning. There are also all manner of trust issues. And then there are simple matters of efficiency. Computing isn't just about cycles; it needs associated data and moving that around takes bandwidth and time, a concept sometimes called "data gravity."

Debates over cloudbursting, though, obscure a broader point.

Cloudbursting debates are really about the dynamic shifting of workloads. Indeed, in their more fevered forms, they suggest movement of applications from one cloud to another in response to real-time market pricing. The reasoned response to this sort of vision is properly cool, not because it isn't a reasonable rallying point on which to set sights and even architect for, but because it's not a practical and credible near- or even mid-term objective.

What is both useful and achievable in the near-term is portability across clouds and hybrid management, perhaps not involving dynamic workload migration—at least in practice—but in the ability to deploy an application on one cloud, or in a virtualized data center, and then be able to move that application to a different cloud at a future point. In the context of enterprise applications, this includes considerations such as carrying over the certifications of software vendors from one cloud to another.

Voltaire supposedly once said *"Le mieux est l'ennemi du bien"* — the better is the enemy of the good. Over the longer-term I'd argue that the better should indeed be the goal, with computing interoperability and portability across multiple dimensions an important part of that advance. However, for more interesting and closer-in time horizons, I think we do ourselves a disservice by obsessing too much with "automagical" workload shifting when what we *really* care about is the ability to just move from one place to another if a vendor isn't meeting our requirements or is trying to lock us in.

How clouds move beyond virtualization

We've already covered some of the nuts-and-bolts of how virtualization relates to clouds at an infrastructure level. But that's only part of the story.

There are two ways to think about the differences between virtualization and cloud. The first is in terms of different mindsets and approaches to IT operations. The other is to consider specific features and capabilities.

Consider the "big picture" aspect first. Mary Johnston Turner, research vice president of enterprise system management software at market researcher IDC, contrasted virtualization and cloud at the 2011 IDC Directions conference. She described virtualization as providing the "underpinning for cloud" while she described cloud as going "beyond virtualization to focus on services and consumption."

What does this mean exactly? In their book *Visible Ops Private Cloud*, Andi Mann, Kurt Milne, and Jeanne Morain write that it's a "shift from framing virtualization expansion goals based on footprint and consolidation metrics to offering business-optimized services. Services that meet user needs will drive adoption. Widespread adoption is critical to driving cloud economics."

This is done by designing a catalog of standardized services—think of them as application or development environments—and offering them to consumers, such as developers, through a low-touch self-service interface. Access to these services is controlled by policy, as is the runtime management (such as patching) of these environments after they are deployed.

Virtualization management, and the ecosystem of third-party management products and add-ons which have grown up around virtualization over time, certainly bring a degree of order and process to virtualized environments. Their goal is to reduce what is sometimes called "VM sprawl" resulting from proliferating unmanaged virtual machines. However, policy, lifecycle management, and standardized workflows are often more fundamentally baked into cloud solutions.

Furthermore, hybrid cloud solutions which operate independently of the underlying virtualization layer can span hypervisors from different vendors and other platforms such as public clouds, allowing management and policy to be extended over a broader and more heterogeneous set of resources.

At IDC Directions, Turner also showed data on the adoption of "critical cloud management building blocks" which reflected "the percentage of IT decision makers reporting their organization is/plans widespread or selective production use of all technology."

Unsurprisingly, virtualization management was the most common current or planned technology. It was present to some degree in about 70 percent of cases with modest (a few percentage points) growth in penetration forecast by 2012. Automation/orchestration and self-service portals were the next most common building blocks, growing from about 40 percent of organizations to over 50 percent. Service management/service catalogs came next; end-to-end performance/ availability management and consumption metering came last in terms of adoption with only about 30 percent anticipating metering even by 2013.

This data is consistent with my observations. A certain amount of automation and self-service can be put in place to augment virtualization but it's with service management and catalogs that IT operations really begin looking like a cloud provider to their internal consumers. This is the point at which we stop thinking so much in terms of managing servers and more in terms of operating IT-as-a-service.

Real world applications for private cloud by Andi Mann

Andi Mann is a longtime mate of mine from my analyst days when he was an IT industry analyst with Enterprise Management Associates (EMA). He's currently Vice President of Strategic Solutions at enterprise IT management software vendor, CA.

Originally posted on October 6, 2011.

Website: http://pleasediscuss.com/andimann/

Twitter: @andimann

Not surprisingly, since the release of my new book, *Visible Ops Private Cloud*, I have been talking with a lot of people about how to deploy private cloud, where to start, what to avoid, etc. So far, the most common question has been, "What type of existing workloads are organizations putting into private cloud environments today—and what are they avoiding?"

So I thought I would jot down some of my answers, specifically related to 'cloud-migrant' services, as opposed to 'cloud-native' services—and without getting too hung up on whether the use cases are 100 percent cloud or not!

One recurrent use case is to provide dynamic desktop allocation, especially for education and projects use cases. A number of schools, universities, training centers, and even some larger enterprises, have adopted private cloud to allocate servers, clients, applications and data for reusable desktop systems.

This seems especially prevalent for short-term learning facilities, repeatable one-off classroom systems, training/demo labs at conventions (or user groups), and contractor setup. It is also similar to the executive briefing centers and 'demos on demand' that many software sales organizations (like CA Technologies) use.

Another service-based use case I have seen in several universities is self-service access for students and faculty, using pooled resources, not only for application services but also for full virtual desktop infrastructure (VDI) desktop allocation.[39]

I have seen this in other enterprises too—most notably for home-source process workers (e.g. call center, data entry)—but mostly as a proof-of-concept, not a large-scale production deployment.

However, most cloud-migrant workloads I see deployed to private clouds today still tend to be server-based. Most of these are at 'Phase 1' in the Visible Ops Private Cloud—a reorientation of virtualization deployments to pilot a private cloud that works, proving results, gaining skills, and hopefully measuring opportunities. It is still focused on servers, not services, but provides a vital part of the learning curve toward private cloud.

For example:

- Development/Test/Quality Assurance servers: 3-tier LAMP[40] stacks (Application/Database/Web server), but also LAMP components, integrated development environments, source code management tools, etc. (which often results in applications that run on a private cloud in production)

- Collaboration servers: especially Microsoft SharePoint, but also Web-based collaboration services like team chat servers, content repositories, blogs, wikis, and project management tools

- Engineering servers: I have seen a number of engineering firms move their design project systems (especially computer aided design (CAD) tools) into private clouds so engineers can fire up new design projects on-demand

---

[39] VDI typically consists of desktop images running on servers and managed by the IT organization rather than running on a local desktop. This "virtual desktop" is then delivered to a PC or "thin client" device. There are many variants and wrinkles but, as a general rule, VDI is used to reduce administrative overhead for standardized desktops used for well-defined functions.

[40] LAMP stands for Linux, Apache (Web server), MySQL (database), and Perl/Python/ PHP (Web programming languages). Essentially, it's shorthand for a standard Web software stack running on the Linux operating system.

- Web servers: popular for marketing teams who can fire up their own Web servers, especially for short-term and/or localized promotions & campaigns

- Analytics servers: short-term number crunching of 'big data' (including business intelligence applications) in medical research, social marketing, pharmaceutical research, higher education, financial, logistics, etc.

The workloads that are less suited to private cloud deployment are harder to identify, because it requires positive evidence of absence, so my thoughts here are much more anecdotal. I do see Chief Information Officers (CIO) push back on migrating 'core' applications, even to private clouds, citing lack of confidence, performance concerns, potential security and compliance issues, and lack of return on investment (ROI). I would not agree these are always good reasons, but they can be, and are certainly understandable.

In my opinion, private cloud is not ideally suited to relatively large, static, predictable, and resource-saturating workloads—think Enterprise Resource Planning or Data Warehouse. After all, used internally such applications are almost never deployed 'on demand'; they are rarely if ever 'multi-tenant'; they have no real benefit from an 'infinitely scalable' infrastructure; and are mostly viewed as a cost of doing business, without any 'resource measurement' or chargeback.

(There are certainly good arguments to deploy these applications on a public cloud, as 'cloud-native' services using SaaS, to outsource them to a non-cloud third-party, or to just virtualize them–even with 1:1 virtualization–without the other trappings of cloud. Such alternatives could deliver better cost savings, higher up-time, faster disaster recovery (DR), and other benefits. However, I think the upside of putting such applications in a private cloud is less apparent.)

That said, I do think that we will see more and more strategic services —as opposed to project servers—deployed in both private and public cloud as it matures. In fact, recent data from market researcher IDC suggests CIOs that are adopting private cloud will migrate many core applications in the coming years. Moreover, some of the more advanced customers I talk with are already doing this, although they are by far in the minority.

Either way, I will be very interested to see how this all pans out.

Beyond ad hoc: Four steps to building a cloud

To give a flavor for how an organization might start building a cloud, consider this methodology based on an approach published in *Visible Ops Private Cloud: From Virtualization to Private Cloud in 4 Practical Steps* by Kurt Milne, Managing Director of the IT Process Institute, along with Andi Mann and Jeanne Moran. The approach was developed based on a survey of over thirty private cloud deployments. This chapter leverages material from a series of white papers that Milne prepared for Red Hat based on this study, book, and mutually-developed content. The focus here is on IaaS, although that will often be the operational foundation for a PaaS, which is more focused on offering services to internal developers and those who support them.

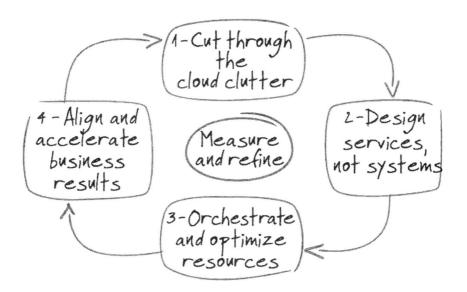

Some new technologies make their way into organizations at the periphery. Perhaps they perform some specific task that is outside of the day-to-day concerns of IT management. Perhaps they're an ad hoc tool of some sort—useful but not part of any formal workflows or procedures. Perhaps they increase efficiency in a way which can be adopted incrementally one server or one group of applications at a time.

In the early days, virtualization mostly fell into this latter category. During the early 2000s, many companies anxiously sought ways to avoid purchasing servers and other IT gear. Server virtualization fit the bill perfectly. Because so many servers (especially those running Microsoft Windows) were woefully underutilized,[41] virtualization was a way to let one physical box do the work of many. And, importantly in the context of that time, virtualization delivered savings even if it was rolled out piecemeal to avoid cutting purchase orders for new servers. As virtualization has become more widespread, IT shops have started approaching it more strategically. But it started out as a tactical, cost-cutting move.

However, not all technologies lend themselves to ad hoc use—at least without causing more problems down the road than they solve. Cloud computing falls into this camp. That's not to say that it can't be brought on board in an evolutionary way—in fact, doing so is often a best practice. However, building an on-premise cloud is usually best done systematically. In addition, while the informal use of public clouds can make sense under some circumstances, it's important to ensure that confidential data is properly secured and that the development environment is consistent with whatever will be used for the application in production. I'll discuss security and compliance in more detail in the context of the next section: Operating a Cloud.

There's no single approach to "properly" adopt a cloud within an organization. It's more important to establish some deliberate process than it is to follow a particular approach. With that said, I'm going to structure this discussion around the framework developed by ITPI. It's fairly lightweight, is based on discussions with organizations who

---

[41] Microsoft Windows running on servers inherited much of the architecture and behaviors of the desktop operating system from which it derived. And the desktop had been designed with one user running one application as its design center. Linux and Unix (the other primary server operating systems) on the other hand, had long been intended to support multiple users and applications running at the same time. As a result, they came with an elaborate toolbox to let multiple workloads run side-by-side and thereby keep utilization up. They weren't nearly as dependent on the arrival of server virtualization as was Windows. (Though they too benefited from it over time.)

have begun implementing clouds, and dovetails nicely with the experiences of Red Hat's services organization.

It's natural to equate process with heavyweight process and heavyweight process with bureaucracy and analysis paralysis. That's certainly not the intent here. Rather, it's to recognize that by bridging IT silos, automating actions, and providing self-service to users, cloud computing delivers a powerful tool to make your IT infrastructure more flexible and responsive to the business. But wielding that tool effectively just takes a bit of upfront planning.

Cut through the cloud clutter

The goal in this phase is to refocus your initial virtualization efforts on skills and competencies that support cloud deployments. The initial discovery pilot phase will enable identification of challenges, requirements, and key metrics that will prepare you for the larger cloud implementation. Your mantra for these activities is, "Get ready for dynamic workloads." You should set end goals for your cloud deployment. You should start laying the groundwork for building shared resource pools and for managing mobile and transitory workloads.

Design cloud services, not systems

Part of the thinking behind on-premise clouds is to offer users fast access to computing resources similar to those offered by commodity third-party cloud providers. However, deploying raw compute resources, either on internal private or external public resource pools, is the lowest common denominator in cloud. The key to cloud success and to minimizing shadow IT is not just speeding up delivery of servers, network, storage, and other computing resources, but also changing what IT offers.

Users are thrilled to get self-service access to cloud services within 15 minutes. But success for cloud initiatives requires joining self-service cloud access with the traditional enterprise IT need for governance, security, and compliance, as well as world-class service delivery and business continuity. A thoughtful service-design approach that shifts focus from resources to delivery and consumption of IT as a service can help meet both user and IT requirements.

A service-design approach includes understanding business objectives, detailing specific user needs, defining services that meet those needs, and defining the functional and technical specifications needed to deliver those services. It also includes creating an IT "factory" used to build and deploy workloads in simple or complex cloud environments both at internal and external resource locations. These processes require clearly defined policies which specify what, how, where, and when workloads are deployed, whether to deploy in public or on-premise clouds, static virtual environments, or even physical dedicated servers.

Optimize and automate IT in the cloud

The cloud computing buzz often centers on giving users self-service on-demand access to various IT services. The promise is that building a private or hybrid cloud enables users to deploy, scale, and redeploy resources as needed. The flexibility can both dramatically increases business agility and improve resource utilization in the data center.

But what about after the workload is deployed? Who maintains and updates the cloud? How does IT ensure ongoing security and compliance?

The reality is that while private cloud utilizes virtualized resources, it is built, run, and governed differently than the static virtualized data center. As a result, IT must address unique run-time challenges such as shared resources, massive scalability, standardized systems management, and hybrid and heterogeneous solutions.

Understanding and addressing these differences is critical for cloud success.

Accelerate business results with your cloud

Frequently, IT capabilities are needed to enable new business initiatives. When IT is in the critical path to revenue, speed matters. *A lot*. In the past, lead times for requesting and receiving IT resources from central IT were too long. As a result, developers and IT staff inside the business units often worked around IT to procure shadow IT resources.

A hybrid cloud implementation can remove much of the typical IT friction associated with growth and innovation efforts. But cloud offers more than speed. Cloud can improve utilization of computing assets and can increase workflow efficiency for a wide range of IT operational processes.

Overall, hybrid cloud solutions are a better way to run IT. These solutions can help shift users' perception of IT from an inhibitor to enabler of business results.

But the cloud's "better, faster, cheaper" value proposition has a critical dependency: broad adoption within the organization. Building something better is a wise use of IT resources only if users adopt what you build. Otherwise, you may be leaving money on the table and undercutting the value IT can offer the business.

Broad adoption occurs when users have enough confidence and trust in the cloud solution that they turn to IT as the preferred service provider. Key activities related to maximizing utilization include optimizing the economics, reshaping user behavior towards IT as a service, streamlining processes to increase collaboration, and shifting towards service-oriented accounting.

How cloud computing will redefine the data center by Judith Hurwitz

Judith S. Hurwitz ,President and CEO of Hurwitz & Associates, Inc., a research and consulting firm focused on emerging technology including

cloud computing, big data, software development, computing management, and security. Judith is a co-author on six retail Dummies titles including: Big Data for Dummies *(Wiley Publishing, 2013),* Hybrid Cloud for Dummies *(Wiley Publishing, 2012),* Cloud Computing for Dummies *(Wiley Publishing 2010),* Service Management for Dummies *(Wiley Publishing, 2009), and* Service Oriented Architecture for Dummies *–first and second editions (Wiley Publishing, 2006, 2009). She is also the author of a business book,* Smart or Lucky? How Technology Leaders Turn Chance into Success *(Jossey-Bass 2011).*

Many organizations are looking at cloud computing as an extension to their traditional data center. It is often viewed as a technique to provide a segregated set of services that can be used for meeting such requirements as supporting peak loads or more easily deploying services on demand. But as with many technology trends, there are unintended and unexpected consequences to the evolution of computing. The cloud will have a dramatic impact on the data center and its evolution.

 In the Hurwitz & Associates book *Hybrid Cloud for Dummies,* we point out that the role of the data center will change in the coming decade. A little history is instructive to understand the impact of these changes. The data center was developed as a fit-for-purpose environment to manage and protect systems of record. In the early days, the data center was optimized for these workloads. Things changed in the 1980s as more systems with different workloads and different operating systems, different hardware, and networks were put in place. The result of this change was that the traditional data center was no longer the optimized and tightly controlled environment that it had been. With this diversity of platforms came complications. The IT operations staff had trouble pleasing its constituents. This resulted in a data center that was ineffective and inefficient in meeting the dynamic changes impacting business.

The result of the inefficiency of the traditional data center has forced companies to adopt cloud services to help alleviate some of the pressure on IT to respond more quickly to business needs. Over the past few years, increasing numbers of small and large corporations have begun using both public and private cloud services alongside their data centers.

Up to this point, however, the role of the traditional data center has not changed very much. Virtualization solutions have somewhat helped to make the data center more efficient, but they have not changed the underlying problems of workload management. But it is inevitable that the role of the data center will not remain static. Rather, the data center will go back to its original purpose: an optimized environment that will support line of business applications that require low latency and high levels of security.

Therefore, there will be fewer hardware platforms, fewer operating systems, and fewer applications that will reside in the traditional data center. In essence, it will become the environment to support the Systems of Record. A second environment based on cloud computing will support dynamic and changing needs of the business – what we can think of as Systems of Engagement.[42] These systems will be cloud-based because they will need to support changing workloads and changing interactions between customers, suppliers, and partners.

---

[42] Author and consultant Geoffrey Moore is credited with coining the "systems of engagement" term. It refers to "the transition from current enterprise systems designed around discrete pieces of information ("records") to systems which are more decentralized, incorporate technologies which encourage peer interactions, and which often leverage cloud technologies to provide the capabilities to enable those interactions." http://www.aiim.org/~/media/Files/AIIM%20White%20Papers/Systems-of-Engagement-Future-of-Enterprise-IT.ashx

These two environments will not exist in isolation from each other. In fact, the redefined data center, with its highly structured Systems of Record, will have to be seamlessly integrated with dynamic and cloud based Systems of Engagement.

The other hybrid: Community clouds

Community clouds were included in the original NIST definition of cloud computing, which has come to be seen as more or less the definitive taxonomy. NIST defined community clouds as cloud infrastructure "provisioned for exclusive use by a specific community of consumers from organizations that have shared concerns (e.g., mission, security requirements, policy, and compliance considerations)." However, as recently as a couple of years ago, it remained something of a theoretical construct—an intriguing possibility with only limited evidence to suggest it would actually happen anytime soon.

That's changed.

It's not that community clouds are everywhere, but we now see concrete commercial examples in the places you'd expect: where there are specific rules and regulations that have to be adhered to and where there are entities that can step up to some sort of supervisory or overseeing role.

For this reason, the federal government is one of the most fertile grounds for the community cloud idea. Certainly government procurement is rife with a veritable alphabet soup of rules, standards, and regulations that must be followed. Indeed, government procurement was one of the driving forces behind the aforementioned NIST definition in the first place. And, in many cases, the policies and process associated with these rules have relatively little overlap with how businesses operate outside of the government sphere.

Furthermore, government agencies aren't wholly independent entities. They've often acted as if they were, to be sure. And one of the big issues with government IT costs historically is that purchases often get made project-by-project, agency-by-agency. That said, initiatives like the 2010 Cloud First Mandate have steered the federal government towards more centralized and shared IT functions. The Cloud First Mandate may not have progressed as quickly as then-US CIO Vivek Kundra initially intended. Nonetheless, it's helped push things along in that direction. (As, no doubt, have budget pressures overall.)

The result is that many agencies are rapidly moving towards a cloud computing model—often using a hybrid approach which bridges internal resources with external GSA providers.

One public cloud specifically catering to the federal government is Amazon's GovCloud which:

> is an AWS Region designed to allow US government agencies and customers to move more sensitive workloads into the cloud by addressing their specific regulatory and compliance requirements. The AWS GovCloud (US) framework adheres to U.S. International Traffic in Arms Regulations (ITAR) requirements. Workloads that are appropriate for the AWS GovCloud (US) region include all categories of Controlled Unclassified Information (CUI), including ITAR, as well as Government oriented publicly available data. Because AWS GovCloud is physically and logically accessible by US persons only, and also supports FIPS 140-2 compliant end points, customers can manage more heavily regulated data in AWS while remaining compliant with federal requirements.

Given the data privacy standards imposed by the HIPAA regulation, healthcare providers also have some specific requirements and concerns when it comes to cloud computing—or, really, IT in general. Nor are these concerns purely academic. In 2011, the Department of Health and Human Services fined two different organizations a total of $5.3 million for data breaches even though those breaches were, arguably, relatively minor. Network World's Brandon Butler offers the example of Optum, the technology division of the UnitedHealth Group:[43]

> [Optum] released its Optum Health Cloud in February as a way for those in the healthcare industry to take advantage of cloud resources. Strict data protection standards regulated by HIPAA, plus a constant pressure to reduce costs and find efficiencies in healthcare management has made community cloud services seem like a natural

---

[43] http://www.networkworld.com/news/2012/030112-are-community-cloud-services-the-256869.html

fit for the industry, says Ted Hoy, senior vice president and general manager of Optum Cloud Solutions. Powered by two data centers owned by Optum, Hoy hopes the community cloud will eventually be able to offer Iaas, SaaS, PaaS for customers.

The service, Hoy says, has differentiating features tailored specifically for the healthcare industry. HIPAA regulations, for example, regulate how secure certain information must be depending on what it is. An e-mail exchange between two doctors about the latest in medical trends needs a different level of protection compared to a communication between a doctor and a patient. Optum worked with Cisco to create security provisions tailor-made for the system that identifies who is entering information, what type of information it is and who has access to it.

It's still early days for community clouds and it's reasonable to question the degree to which they'll expand beyond fairly specific (and relatively obvious) uses such as we're mostly seeing to date. At another level though, I see this as another example of how it's hard to call exactly where workloads are going to end up running and how IT is going to be sourced, which is why industry analysts such as Gartner are making such a big deal about concepts such as Hybrid IT.

Controlling a Cloud

Building cool stuff is great. But remember that prior stat about 70 or 80 percent of spending going towards keeping the lights on at a typical IT department? Well, that should serve as a stark reminder that most of the work (and expense) happens after the light switch is flipped on.

Indeed, cloud computing is as much an operational and management model as it is about initially building a hybrid environment. Some of this model relates to operational management of the infrastructure, whether it's performed by a public cloud provider or by in-house staff. Cloud computing also means managing the applications (and their associated services) that are running in a cloud.

It ain't fire and forget

One way to think about what's different about cloud computing and related enterprise computing transformations is that they embody what MIT's Jeanne Ross calls a "culture of discipline."[44]

> ...the thing we're learning about enterprise architecture is that there's a cultural shift that takes place in an organization, when it commits to doing business in a new way, and that cultural shift starts with abandoning a culture of heroes and accepting a culture of discipline.
>
> Nobody wants to get rid of the heroes in their company. Heroes are people who see a problem and solve it. But we do want to get past heroes sub-optimizing. What companies traditionally did before they started thinking about what architecture would mean, is they relied on individuals to do what seemed best and that clearly can sub-optimize in an environment that increasingly is global and requires things like a single face to the customer.
>
> What we're trying to do is adopt a culture of discipline, where there are certain things that people throughout an enterprise understand are the way things need to be done, so that we actually can operate as an enterprise, not as individuals all trying to do the best thing based on our own experience.

This philosophy is very much in line with the idea that a hybrid cloud moves beyond virtualization by shifting to a services-centric approach. This means offering a standardized catalog of services to users and controlling access to and deployment of those services through policy. In other words, it's about granting access to IT services within a framework of established, consistent policies. A "culture of discipline," if you will, rather than an ad hoc "culture of heroes."

A discipline culture can really streamline the access to IT resources rather than the other way around. Yes, there are consistent controls and policies in place, but self-service access within that framework makes for more agility, not less.

---

[44] http://www.zdnet.com/blog/gardner/mits-ross-on-how-enterprise-architecture-and-it-more-than-ever-lead-to-business-transformation/4463

A discipline of culture doesn't need to mean a culture of "No." In fact, it can make saying "Yes" easier and faster.

This section takes a look at some of the ways in which cloud represents a difference in kind from many traditional IT practices and some of the concerns which cloud operations and management need to address.

One such concern is "security," which can be found at the top of just about any survey asking about inhibitors to cloud computing. As we'll see, security often gets used as a convenient placeholder for lots of things related to managing risk and controlling IT processes. It's also the subject of widespread assumptions which often don't square well with reality.

Some cloud operational aspects are informed by traditional IT practice methodologies such as ITIL—that "discipline" thing. But automation and repeatable best practices are married to a more bottoms-up approach that brings together IT policy with the needs of users accustomed to the low-friction world of cloud consumer services. We'll take a look at how hybrid cloud management bridges these two worlds.

The cloud is breaking down walls in other ways as well. Whereas application developers and IT operators historically worked in largely isolated spheres, cloud computing is part of a general motion towards more integrated functions for which DevOps is one commonly-used shorthand.

At the same time, it's worth remembering that cloud computing still depends on physical servers, disk drives, and networks. Cloud computing architectures still need to consider factors such as how quickly data can move from place to place and how much can be transferred. Ye canna' change the laws of physics.

IT operations in a cloudy world by James Urquhart

James Urquhart is VP of Product Strategy for enStratus. His original post references earlier "Big Rethink" and DevOps series from his former CNET Wisdom of the Clouds blog http://news.cnet.com/ wisdom-of-clouds/.

Twitter: @jamesurquhart

Cloud computing and data center virtualization are both changing the way IT operations are organized, and the toolsets sought to automate operations tasks. Recent conversations with a variety of cloud practitioners have reemphasized this for me, and I wanted to lay out what changes I see coming to the operations space, and why those changes are important when considering your future (or your product's future).

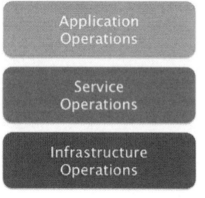

The first thing that I think is critical to identify is that there are really three elements to IT operations in a world where IT is delivered as a service:

I think of these three categories in the following way:

Infrastructure operations (or "InfraOps") is the management of the base physical systems (such as physical servers, networking and storage), and usually the virtualized representations of those resources—though not always, as you'll see below. Included in this infrastructure are the management systems focused on managing resource allocation at the behest of services and applications.

What is critical to understanding the role of InfraOps is understanding that infrastructure is moving towards a more homogenous model in support of heterogeneous applications and services (a "Big Rethink" concept). If the same core infrastructure is going to host multiple services and applications, it therefore makes sense that a single team of dedicated professionals would watch over that infrastructure, theoretically guaranteeing the ability of that infrastructure to adjust to the demands of its payloads.

Service operations (or "ServiceOps") is then the role that focuses on running the services provided on that infrastructure. For example, the ServiceOps team would own the service catalog and service portal environments, and all of the software systems that define and manage the services offered through those systems.

Why manage services separately from the infrastructure they run on? I usually illustrate this concept with an analogy: think of the data center infrastructure as an iPad, and the services it hosts as "apps." Ultimately, I may move towards a more homogeneous data center infrastructure in support of my services, but I still want a wide ranging choice of service options to select from. Perhaps I build my own infrastructure as a service offering, buy my communications services from a vendor, and my dev/test governance services from another vendor.

Application Automation

Service Automation

Infrastructure Automation

If the data center is hosting multiple services from multiple sources, there will need to be expertise to support the common infrastructure (as mentioned above) and expertise to support each of the services. This means service operations would need to be managed separately from infrastructure operations.

Application Operations (or "AppOps") then is the role that manages the applications themselves, assuring that the application has a place to execute, that it is deployed correctly, and that service level requirements are met throughout the life of the application. AppOps typically is the team that is involved in DevOps activities, and is also the most likely role to find itself working with multiple "clouds" (aka IT service providers) at once.

This is the primary effect of the "Big Rethink" and DevOps: the drive to make the application itself the unit of administration from the application's perspective, rather than the infrastructure on which it runs. To me, this is an exciting change, as it get's application operators out of the business of being "clerks" (e.g. responding to trouble tickets day after day), and into the creative business of architecting, implementing, and maintaining application operations automation.

(For the more technical readers, I should note that today, many so-called "cloud infrastructure" tools tightly couple physical resource allocation to an "infrastructure as a service" software system. The problem I see with that is that it means the infrastructure can only be used with that service offering, or other services that utilize the same management and user interface systems as that offering. I believe that the "service" component of IaaS will eventually be decoupled from the actual infrastructure automation for that reason.)

By the way, some of you may have picked up on a very interesting point that can be derived from this breakdown of operations. The separation of operations roles basically denotes the separation of operations automation systems that should be deployed in an cloud ecosystem; the same three elements are involved:

Now, it will take time for these roles to appear in many organizations, but I find it hard to picture a different breakdown that will allow for (a) maximum flexibility and efficiency in infrastructure usage, and (b) the separation of concerns that come into play when you have an end user consuming a second party service that is running on a third party's infrastructure—a very reasonable model in the world of cloud computing.

Risk managing the cloud

You've probably heard or read this sound bite: "The Cloud is unsafe." Maybe it was after some large public cloud provider had an outage. Or maybe a bank had a data breach. Or some security researcher identified... well, something that could possibly be connected to some aspect of cloud computing is some way, shape, or form.

Statements like this are meaningless. We might as well say "Cars are unsafe." Unsafe relative to what alternatives and under what circumstances? Unsafe in what way? What benefit do they provide relative to the purported lack of safety?

Similarly in cloud computing, "safety" can refer to many different types of risks. Some are specific to using a public cloud provider. Others to outsourced hosting more broadly. Others to the dynamic IT infrastructures with self-service that are part and parcel of cloud computing (whether it's out in a public cloud or within an organization's own physical perimeter). And, truth be told, many of the risks talked about in the context of cloud computing are age-old IT governance concerns—though perhaps traveling under a new name.

Let's take a look at a few of the specific areas to think about and examine how you might mitigate risk.

Approaching public cloud provider risk analysis solely from a classic security perspective is usually the wrong way to think about it. It's expected that large providers have solid skills in physical security; proper disposal of used storage assets, firewall configuration, and prompt vulnerability mitigation should be givens. Due diligence when selecting a public cloud provider is still needed! But bigger and more complicated risks may lurk elsewhere.

For example, where is your data stored? Is it guaranteed to reside in a specific country? Under what circumstances will the service provider provide a third party access to your data—say, through a judicial order? Are they guaranteed to notify you if your data is accessed deliberately or otherwise?

Risks like these are the bigger ones associated with a public cloud provider and may help to guide you toward which applications you keep in-house and which you run on a public cloud provider. The key with this type of analysis is to balance the potential cost, the possibility of a bad event happening, and the expected benefit. Making such determinations isn't easy; low-probability events with costly outcomes are notoriously difficult to properly account for in all manner of fields. However, the goal, at a minimum, should be to avoid making potentially costly decisions that are at least somewhat likely to happen.

Another cloud provider risk falls under the term "portability." Portability covers a number of dimensions but the basic idea is that if you write applications or store data on one provider, you want to be able to move to another provider as easily as possible. Perhaps the first provider failed, wasn't providing an agreed-to level of service, or simply started to cost more than some alternative.

Barriers to portability are most evident in the case of public cloud providers who offer programming interfaces or other provider-specific hooks which increase the work and cost to move to another provider. I touched on this earlier in the API discussion. However, the same logic can apply to technology stacks within an internal datacenter. Hybrid cloud computing management that spans both a wide range of internal infrastructure as well as public clouds helps provide a degree of portability. Cross-platform interoperability has historically been best provided by open source and open standards and we should expect this same dynamic to play out in cloud computing.

Another area of potential risk comes about through self-service, one of the defining features that lets a cloud computing architecture deliver resources to users quickly. The basic issue is this: provisioning IT resources to users has historically happened through well-defined workflows within IT operations. The process might take a while— weeks or months even—but it has at least the appearance of careful control. (I say appearance because one result was often the establishment of a "Shadow IT" which had few or no controls at all.)

With the shift to self-service, the challenge is therefore to realize the speed and low friction of this new operational model without simply throwing out all the governance baked into the old one. One approach is to deliver self-service under the umbrella of a rich policy framework. This means authenticating users, deciding on the types of resources they can request, and determining where those resources can then be physically deployed. For example, development workloads may only be able to run in some places while production workloads are only able to run in others.

However, beyond a policy framework, it's also important to maintain the same application lifecycle management processes within a cloud computing environment as it is with a more traditional IT environment. Indeed, because clouds are designed to scale quickly, be more responsive to changing business needs, and generally be more dynamic, it's more important than ever for control to be built in rather than ad hoc. Automation is at the core of dynamic IT—but it has to be automation that creates standardized builds and monitors those standardized builds for changes. Otherwise, the result can be what has come to be called "VM sprawl" — huge numbers of one-off, unmanaged virtual machines that can send management costs spinning out of control.

The benefits of cloud computing far outweigh its risks—risks that have often been sensationalized based on one-off events. But that's not an excuse for ignoring risk. Rather, one must understand and mitigate it.

Cloud security: Excerpts from an interview with Richard Morrell

Richard Morrell is Red Hat's Cloud Evangelist in Europe. Richard has spent more than the the last fifteen years working in Open Source. He started out working with Linuxcare and VA Linux in San Francisco around the same time that Red Hat was incorporated. He joined Red Hat in 2010. The following is summarized from a 2012 interview.

Website: http://cloudevangelist.org/

Twitter: @EMEACloudGuy

The cloud is as safe as the vendor, the controls that are put in place, and also by the thought and the governance that goes into the development and the architecture of the systems that are deployed on cloud.

If we can look at the trailblazers in cloud, who have started to move those applications and services into the virtualized environment, into the new world of elastic computing, we have a compelling story to tell. But it needs people to start thinking about being courageous enough to start building the internal controls and processes to be able to think about the workloads they want to move to cloud to keep them safe.

What we're doing in cloud security is really no different from the security controls that we've used in the SOA [Service Oriented Architecture] environments traditionally within data centers and with on-premise data. What we need to think about is the cost in ownership of how we actually get to cloud, and once we get there, the management controls and the governance risk control piece that we as

IT professionals are dear to as part and parcel of standard business-as-usual activities.

The security standards in cloud have been dovetailed into a mishmash of risk issues, with which people like the Cloud Security Alliance are critically involved. We have been working very, very closely with the CSA now for quite some time, and in past lives I've been pushing and promoting the cloud security matrices. If none of you are already aware of this, I suggest you Google the words "security matrix" and "CSA," and you will find that there are over 80 individuals working out there, from the Basel, PCI-DSS, ISO, and the open-source community, building levels of controls that you can push to your applicable workloads. This applies to whatever vertical you happen to be working in, whether it's health, whether it's finance. It enables you to get a standing start in understanding what you need to be able to say to your CIO or your CFO with regards to who needs to sign off against what, and also the controls and matrices that you need to push against the applicable standards you're building.

It's really up to individuals who consume technologies like the latest open source programming languages to ensure that when you go to cloud that you work with your vendor to ensure that you have the latest, greatest patches working there. And also have a complex risk register so you understand, potentially, what that means from a data leakage or a data privacy perspective.

We can't lose focus on the fact that, at the end of the day, you need to be able to be auditable. In the US and further afield, we have the SAS 70 certification, which is really no more than an accounting standard. We hope it will be surpassed by the sort of standards that the Cloud Security Alliance is pushing and promoting, and also the PCI-DSS and Basel piece where companies are actually looking to make revenue from applications hosted either on a public/private hybrid model or directly on public cloud providers.

I regularly stand up at conferences and I don't tend to conform to the norm and the first question I ask the crowded room is, "Who wants to go to jail first?" I'm met with a lot of white, ashen faces.

When you're working with your chosen provider, don't be afraid to ask them for the levels of both security controls and also the physical and mandatory access controls that they have built into their architecture. They should be able to provide it. If a provider just comes back to you saying oh we're secure or here's my SAS 70 certificate that's not enough. You need to be able to push and promote the fact that you're also talking to other cloud vendors that can do it bigger and better. Please, can I have the right information?

You also need to be able to ensure that the data that you're moving to cloud is secure. Think about the level of risk that your company is willing to be exposed to. Also, is it possible that you can work with your trusted vendors to be able to have a hybrid model where you can tunnel databases from your data center to a cloud provider without exposing that level of risk?

The other thing is this is fun. This is enabling us to change the paradigm of computing. Red Hat is a trusted vendor. We have the ability now to help you get to where you want to go. It's like a level of adolescence now and we're here to help you get to that next level.

It's not just about security

Cloud computing needs governance. Which is to say that cloud computing needs processes, policies, and procedures. In a way, this is no different from IT more broadly. But virtualization, dynamically moving workloads, and an increased reliance on third parties for many types of IT functions mean that well thought-out and documented processes, policies, and procedures tend to be more important in cloud computing than with a more static and manual environment.

The traditional view of security as being largely about having a well-defended perimeter is an increasingly obsolete concept.

Security procedures and technology are part of governance, but governance is a broader concept.

Legal and regulatory procedures, transparency, service levels, indemnification, notification, and portability are all part of this bigger picture, especially as the discussion widens to include public cloud infrastructure providers and software-as-a-service vendors. It's all about mitigating risk associated with suppliers (whether supplying software for on-premise IT or supplying infrastructure in a public cloud).

Consistency is one of the most important ways to support well-governed cloud architectures whether on-premise, public, or a hybrid architecture.

Consistency refers to having a runtime environment (such as an operating system or middleware) that is common across different clouds, private and public, as well as virtualization platforms and physical servers. This allows an application that uses those runtimes —written in Linux, Java, PHP, or whatever—to thereby run in both places. The bottom line is that the user of that application or its developer should not generally care where the application is deployed. (Of course, the IT operations people need to know where workloads are running as well as specifying upfront where different workloads are allowed to run.)

One of the ways that consistency breaks down is that public clouds can encourage ad hoc development which doesn't necessarily comply with an organization's standards for applications run on-premise. This may be fine for prototyping or other work that is throwaway by design or for applications only intended to ever run on a specific provider. However, it's far too easy for prototypes to evolve into something more—as often happened in the case of early visual programming languages—and the result is applications that either have to be rewritten or that may have support, reliability, or scalability issues down the road.

Consistency goes beyond just technical factors though. Consistency between on-premise and public cloud environments also requires that the full runtime—including the applications running on it—be supported and certified by the same software developers and others wherever it's running, a commitment that is as much about business relationships as technical ones.

The intention here isn't to harp on the potential downsides of using public clouds. The benefits offered by public cloud infrastructures operated by companies like Amazon and software-as-a-service offered by someone like Salesforce.com are well documented. In the case of infrastructure, they allow rapid experimentation and expansion. SaaS applications can often be brought online more quickly than conventional on-premise software and they thereby can start delivering business value faster.

The reality is that cloud computing in some form will happen throughout all organizations whether it's the evaluation and adoption of a new customer relationship management platform through a formal IT process, the ad hoc use of public cloud infrastructure by developers, or the "bursting" of an on-premise cloud to a public cloud to gain temporary capacity. Especially given the importance of properly securing data and minimizing lock-in to specific third-party provider, it's critical to bring cloud computing activity that involves corporate data or production applications under a common governance umbrella.

So better to acknowledge that reality and, to the degree possible, make it an explicit part of overall IT governance. An IT organization might, for example, freely allow personal devices to access corporate e-mail but put in place mechanisms such as tokens, which add a layer of security to that access. As one CIO told me, perhaps the most important process is to involve users in formulating the policies rather than creating an IT vs. everyone else dynamic.

Cloud computing isn't "risky" any more than IT, more broadly, is risky. Rather, like all IT activities, cloud computing projects should be undertaken in a way which both mitigates risk and considers those projects in the context of IT as a whole. Cloud computing projects and IT activities more generally must also take into account the ultimate objective: to support the business in a way that balances costs with benefits.

Red Hat's Chris Wells on hybrid cloud management

Excerpts from an interview with Chris Wells, product marketing manager for CloudForms, Red Hat's open hybrid cloud management product. Chris runs product marketing for Red Hat's cloud management products. Chris came to Red Hat from Quest Software, where he managed over fifty of their key enterprise products.

Can you just give us a high level view of what CloudForms is and what a hybrid cloud management product does generally?

When we take a look at Red Hat CloudForms, it's really doing several different things for you. The whole goal is we want to give customers the ability to build out and manage their own private clouds and then go into a hybrid cloud model to be able to leverage a public cloud infrastructure. We also want the ability to go across heterogeneous infrastructures. We really want to give customers the choice of where they're going to run things in the cloud, meaning that they want to be able to pick whether it's physical machines or different types of hypervisors. And then also give them a choice of different types of public cloud providers.

When we take a look at CloudForms, it's fundamentally about not just being able to be able to run systems on different types of infrastructure, but it's also about being able to manage the applications that will then run in that infrastructure and do all of the traditional systems management tasks around that. Patching systems, provisioning systems, configuring systems.

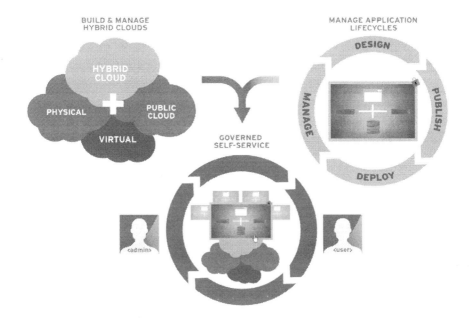

CloudForms overview showing main functional elements.

So at Red Hat, we believe that if you want to get to your own private or hybrid cloud environment, you want to offer an ability such as self-service provisioning. So, fundamentally, you've got to be able to manage across multiple different types of infrastructure, as well as manage different types of applications that run in that cloud infrastructure.

Then there's a whole policy that you can put in front of it to decide who can do it, what kind of access, what the system dependencies are so, as an IT infrastructure team, you still have control of your infrastructure.

I assume that this is where you see a difference with a private or hybrid cloud that's governed by IT and the shadow IT by credit card you see with Amazon?

I've talked to quite a few customers. I'm talking to centralized IT teams. They're nervous about shadow IT that's in other parts of their business units and organization, because they know, at the end of the day, that they're going to be held accountable, the centralized IT teams, for the security of data, the availability of infrastructure, even if it's being done by a shadow IT organization. They know it's eventually going to come back onto them. They're trying to figure out ways to give their internal customers that flexibility that a public cloud provider would provide but have all those controls.

There are analogues to the whole consumerization of IT, whether it's iPhones or Android phones or tablets or what have you. The best-of-breed IT organizations really don't want to just say, "No, you can't use any of this stuff, even if it makes your jobs easier, faster, more efficient." But on the other hand, they really just can't say, "Hey, sure, put the corporate data on your laptop. No big deal."

I think what's changed is we've had some cultural changes in IT over the last few years. Whereas I'd argue 10 years ago, centralized IT teams were very rigid, very structured. You did it their way or the highway. And what's changed? You talked about the consumerization of IT. You've had people walk in with their smartphones and say, "Hey, I need to have this smartphone access our email." And IT now can't just ignore that demand. On the infrastructure side, what's changing is that the public cloud providers, which have come online over the last few years, have set a new bar that IT has to answer. I have an option. I can take my corporate credit card and go get a virtual machine on a public cloud provider very quickly and very easily, and if my centralized IT team can't give me that service, I'll go someplace else.

So the point is, the IT teams have to react. And they're looking for ways to be able to do that that allows them to leverage existing investments they already have in their organization, because they can't throw out existing infrastructure. But yeah, it does give them that ability to be more agile and more flexible, more responsive to what the business wants.

Self-service is really a pretty fundamental aspect of cloud computing, whether we're talking public clouds or private clouds. A lot of the time, we hear this expressed in the form of users having access to a service catalog. What does that mean?

The easiest way to think of a service catalog is it's just a listing of all of the applications or resources that you want to be able to give someone access to. Ideally, you want to have this on-demand web page or portal that someone can go to and say, "Hey, look, I need a database instance or an application server instance or a web server," or whatever it happens to be. I think the easiest use case is probably around developers. If I'm a developer, I'm going to be spinning up a sandbox [an isolated environment to "play" in] for an application server very quickly. I want to get access to it to get my job done. But it may only live for a relatively short amount of time, because once I finish that development or test whatever, I just want to throw it away.

Traditional IT process today, if I'm a developer, I've got to put in a self-service ticket. Maybe I've got to send an email. It's got to go to someone. It might take them a couple of days to meet the request, get the hardware, get the software. Most companies I talk to say that could be a three, four week process before I have my sandbox.

How does this service catalog get built in a cloud management product like Red Hat's CloudForms?

The way we would do it inside of CloudForms is that what you're going to start with, once you have all your hybrid infrastructure in place, you're going to focus on is creating what we call the Application Blueprint. The Application Blueprint is the outline of all the software and configuration that you want to be able to provide to someone.

You're also going to define all the policy that goes around it, like who has access to it, what the application itself has access to, what kind of infrastructure it is allowed to run on. Can it run on a public cloud provider? Does it run in a test environment? A virtual environment? Does it run production on a physical environment? You're going to define all these requirements.

And then, finally, you're going to actually publish into the service catalog. The easiest way to think of a service catalog is to just think of it as a web portal, a web page that's going to have a list of all the things that an end user is allowed to have access to.

It could look as simple as, "Here are all of our different flavors of a base virtual machine. It has just an operating system in it." You could layer it on with middleware and application tools. It could have a database, it could have a web server. It's really whatever you want to define.

I think a lot of people would think of that as a golden image, if you will. To be able to click on that and get a golden image. That's conceptually what it is. The way that we do it in CloudForms is a little bit different than a pure golden image, but it's the same kind of concept.

How is it different, a golden image and CloudForms?

It's different in that most people like images because when you've built an image and you have all of the content and configuration in it, it has two really big advantages. One advantage is you've got it all defined in one file so you've got that gold master that you're going to build everything from so it's very repeatable. The other thing that's very nice about an image is that it's very fast to deploy. It's basically all executable and ready to go, so when it comes time to deploy and provision a new system you can do it very fast. The real downside to an image is an image is like a big blob. It's a big file, if you will. So if you need to go in and make any changes to it, like make a small, one percent change to update a particular software package for a security concern or something, you essentially have to update the whole image. You can't just manage that one little piece.

CloudForms uses a template. Think of it almost like a configuration file that basically outlines all the different components that are going to go into it, that always goes out and grabs the freshest software, if you will, the software that's the most up to date security wise, package wise, whatever you've tested and certified. You kind of get the best of both worlds. You're not having to manage really large files and images yet the speed to deploy is very fast. It's a very automated process that you can repeat again and again and again.

This is really the idea that you're bringing together the self-service ease of Amazon and other public clouds with IT compliance and governance, all that kind of good stuff.

Absolutely. I think that's what the hybrid cloud is all about. The hybrid cloud is all about being able to leverage all of the infrastructure that's appropriate for that job, whether it be your internal infrastructure or external infrastructure, but having all the policy and control around it.

Investment and ROI in the Cloud

Increased agility. Faster time-to-market. Increased business value. Phrases like these pepper cloud computing marketing literature. Cloud computing concepts are more focused on IT as a business enabler than on simply making IT cost less. But that doesn't mean costs don't matter. They always do.

The trick, then, is to develop an understanding of how the businesses benefits might be quantified. The resulting analysis will mostly consist of soft costs, which are often justifiably viewed with suspicion— especially if they come from a vendor trying to sell you something. Nonetheless, they're a good starting point. After all, the alternative is to assume that the benefit is worth nothing. And, as a business school professor of mine was fond of saying "Zero is a very precise number."

Some of the metrics that you might use for your analysis include:

Time to deploy a new service (application). One of the main features of cloud delivery models is that users are given self-service access to computing resources. On-demand provisioning can dramatically decrease the time needed to kick off a new project or to ramp up work on an existing one. At the same time, self-service takes place under a managed, policy-based framework so the IT department can maintain appropriate control over usage patterns. While a soft benefit, this speed and agility can be quantified through a combination of productivity measures.

Standard Operating Environments. Research from Gartner shows that an average of 80 percent of mission-critical application service downtime is directly caused by human error or process failure. A significant portion can be attributed to change management and configuration management, which the centralization of policy and workflow controls in a cloud computing infrastructure can help reduce. Gartner goes on to note that downtime can tarnish a company's image and reputation. While this can be hard to quantify, downtime can also cause a company to miss out on orders or may force overtime to make up for lost productivity.

Admin to server ratio. One of the big efficiency differences between a public cloud provider and traditional enterprise IT lies in how many servers (or virtual machines) an administrator can manage. For traditional enterprise IT, a few dozen servers per admin is a fairly typical number. For a large cloud provider, a ratio of servers per admin into the thousands is not unheard of. Much of the difference can be attributed to the high level of standardization which large cloud providers drive into their operations. While it won't typically be possible for an enterprise to adopt such cookie cutter practices, a private or hybrid cloud can nonetheless provide a means to develop and deploy a more standardized catalog of services to users, thereby reducing the amount of one-off work that admins need to perform to keep images updated and patched.

If we broaden the discussion to explicitly include public cloud services of various kinds, a number of interesting angles appear. The most obvious is the trading off of capital expenditures, CAPEX, for operating expenses, OPEX. You no longer have to buy servers—or at least not as many of them—but you have to rent them on an ongoing basis.

Is this a good tradeoff? Well, it depends. The initial hurdle which many organizations face when doing this sort of analysis is that they often don't have a good handle on their internal IT cost. I'd argue that one of the benefits of public clouds (even for organizations that don't use them) is that they encourage this sort of benchmarking. Which is a good thing.

In general though, the results suggest that we can draw certain generalizations about public cloud vs. on-premise IT costs.

Many large organizations run IT operations that are competitive with public clouds—at least on the basis of cost. For example, the aforementioned 2009 "Clearing the Air on Cloud Computing" study by management consultants McKinsey found that "current cloud computing services are generally not cost effective for larger enterprises." Various assumptions in this report were widely criticized at the time. However, a wealth of anecdotal evidence in the time since suggests that McKinsey's basic point mostly holds; large data center operations running generally well-understood and predictable workloads can be as cheap or cheaper than public clouds.

An increasingly common meme is "Rent the peak and own the base." In other words, use your own servers for baseline loads and use public clouds to handle the spikes—or new applications whose usage characteristics you don't understand well yet. A poster child for this approach is social gaming company Zynga.

That said, a few sizable companies have gone all-in on public cloud. Internet movie and TV subscription service Netflix is perhaps the best known example of a firm that's made the strategic decision to move just about everything to a public cloud (Amazon Web Services in their case). The strongest argument for this approach is probably focus. Companies can do lots of things in-house, but they're generally best only doing those things for which they bring competitive differentiation. Netflix has decided that running servers—as opposed to the code and data on those servers—isn't a differentiator for them. It doesn't hurt that, in Netflix' case, the number of subscribers provides a more direct linkage between revenue and IT capacity consumed than is the case with many firms.[45]

And this is ultimately one of the great benefits that public cloud services can bring. Sure, if you're a smallish business, a public cloud provider is probably going to offer you computing at a lower hourly cost than you can achieve yourself. Or an online SaaS vendor will be able to save you money relative to installing and operating your own Microsoft Exchange server.

However, whether private or public or (as is increasingly the case) hybrid, organizations would be well advised to not only focus on quantifying OPEX and/or CAPEX reductions but also to consider how

---

[45] In financial markets, companies are routinely willing to spend a bit more on average to align their revenue sources and their payment obligations in an attempt to reduce risk—not that doing so always works of course.

the agile and flexible delivery of IT services via the cloud can help the organization execute on its mission—whatever that may be.

IT as business enabler

Historically, users viewed IT departments as being staffed by people who ran the basic infrastructure "plumbing," but were inflexible when it came to doing anything new, and were generally far more of an inhibitor to the business than an enabler. That take was at least mildly unfair in most cases, but it was grounded in certain realities.

For most organizations, IT was primarily focused on a fairly standard —if hardly standardized—set of tasks. Functions like enterprise resource planning, financials, human resources, and e-mail all had to work. But they weren't things that especially advantaged the organization most of the time. Yes, it's pretty important to have a working accounting system but few businesses win because they have a better accounting system than they guy down the street.

Today, we often see the same underlying issue presented in the context of the amount of money that companies spend on innovation versus keeping the lights on. The figures and the phrasing depend on which analyst's report you're reading but typical numbers are something like: for every 30 cents spent on doing new things in support of the business, 70 cents gets spent on maintenance and the rest of the routine.

With the important caveat that there's enormous inertia in existing applications, systems, and so forth, I think the situation is changing. Let me point to a number of data points.

First is how cloud computing is widely viewed as an investment to help the business rather than primarily a way to just cut costs (as virtualization primarily was at first).

Take, for example, the results of a survey that Michelle Bailey presented at market research firm IDC's Directions 2011 conference. It found that "response to the business is a significantly more important driver for private cloud adoption than costs." In fact, organizations primarily interested in reducing costs were actually *less* interested in adopting private clouds. Among the drivers cited by those looking to adopt private clouds were: to improve response to changes in workload, to aid in disaster recovery, to improve availability, and to speed deployment time.

Thinking about IT as an organization which can help drive revenue rather than just cost money is also a common theme at CIO-oriented events I attend.

At one 2012 event, the CIO of electronics distributor Avnet talked of using "IT to accelerate profitable growth." He went on to discuss investing in IT for strategic advantage. He didn't dismiss the importance of efficiency. Anything but. However, he discussed efficiency more in the context of being able to support a rapidly changing global business and managing IT sustaining costs to allow for investments in innovation than about cutting the bottom line.

Rob Baxter, the CIO of Shamrock Foods, discussed how the payback for installing a high-definition video conferencing system was "priceless" from a business process perspective. The financial payback from travel savings wasn't bad either: 13 months.

This too was a common theme. Make IT projects successful for the business and the financial benefits will come. Another example came from the CIO of a community college. The school went with a broad-based client virtualization and public cloud e-mail approach to better accommodate a wide range of "bring your own" student devices. But they too saved money compared to their prior internally hosted approach.

Another theme was a more proactive IT group. Bertrand Odinet, the CIO of mining firm Freeport-McMoRan Copper & Gold, described IT as having "to set a vision for the executive team to understand what tech can do. What will differentiate us? Clarity of business imperatives is critical." It's easy to see that, more than ever, CIOs bridge the worlds of operating IT and supporting, even driving, corporate strategy.

Mundane, largely undifferentiated IT functions are often best farmed out to specialists. Payroll is the canonical historical example. It's easy to underestimate the challenges of untangling legacy systems and processes. And governance concerns are not just an excuse to stay on a "business as usual" path. But the fundamental point that IT should focus on where they can add distinct value is valid. Many companies, both historically and today, think they have more unique IT needs than they do. Off-the-shelf software or SaaS should always be at least considered.

What the broader argument about outsourcing undifferentiated IT misses, though, is that for every e-mail or customer relationship management system that would be better moved offsite to a SaaS vendor, there's a new differentiated application or new capability that IT can deliver. And these new applications and capabilities can support or even create new business opportunities. The old functions may be getting less differentiated but new ones taking their place are arguably more central than ever to a company's success.

Best practices for the cloud

Ultimately, there is no single right way to build a cloud on-premise or to procure cloud services from an external cloud provider. Something that's appropriate to build lightweight applications used only by developers may not be appropriate for an application which interacts with live customer credit card data. However, based on experiences with helping customers build and otherwise consume clouds, the following are some of my recommendations ton crafting a savvy cloud strategy based on solid governance principles.

- Software-as-a-Service applications, public cloud resources, and mobile devices of many types are going to be used by people within an organization whether officially sanctioned or otherwise. Therefore, it makes sense for IT to recognize this reality and establish appropriate policies that leverage the flexibility and acquisition ease of cloud resources without compromising the security of data or other aspects of IT governance. For example, IT might, after doing due diligence, create a list of approved public cloud providers in the same manner as many organizations have a list of other approved vendors.

- Recognize that selecting a public cloud provider or hosted application requires the same sort of due diligence that should accompany any outsourcing project to ensure that the selected provider is a trusted destination for your applications and data.

- Even if you have decided to use infrastructure or applications in the cloud, it is critical that you always have a path to exporting or maintaining a regular backup of your data in a usable form. The organization's informational governance policies have to apply to all corporate data, wherever it resides. While these concerns are typically greatest with Software-as-a-Service, understanding where data resides and how it is protected is important in any situation in which you lack direct visibility and control.

- Wherever possible, favor cloud providers which use or can interface to common sets of APIs. However, recognize that cloud computing is a rapidly developing area that doesn't have, nor is likely to develop in the near future, a single set of standards. Use open, hybrid management to enable operability among different clouds.

- Develop a strategy which allows applications and data, to the degree possible, to be moved with the minimum of effort between public cloud providers, from private clouds to public clouds, and from public clouds to private clouds. While transparent movement of resources is not always possible, especially in the case of proprietary applications and platforms hosted by a single provider, the goal should be to maximize mobility and only to give it up when the benefits outweigh the considered risks.

- When initially hosting applications on a public cloud, develop and deploy them with an eye to maintaining a consistent, certified environment across multiple private clouds and public clouds. This will typically be done through a runtime, such as an operating system or middleware, that is certified with your applications and can be deployed across a heterogeneous and hybrid infrastructure.

- While recognizing that individual applications have their own unique circumstances, establish overall policies that define acceptable cloud usage within the organization. These policies should, among other factors, take into account organizational audit requirements and any relevant regulations or industry best practices. These policies should be flexible enough not to prohibit reasonable uses which will happen whether sanctioned or under the radar. Having consistent environments across on-premise and public environments can eliminate much of the uncertainty associated with using a unique, publicly-hosted service.

- Different cloud platforms will be more suitable for some uses than for others. It also makes sense to have some diversity of suppliers as a risk mitigation technique. Nonetheless, you should make an effort to control unwarranted proliferation of platforms, especially to the degree that they are not fully interoperable, if only because of the effort required to monitor all suppliers for continued adherence to your established policies.

- Investigate SaaS solutions primarily for those functions that are relatively standardized, needed by a wide range of organizations, and that are not core to your business (even if they're important). Customer Relationship Management and email are common examples.

- Many of the new governance concerns related to cloud computing primarily relate to public clouds and how they interface with private clouds. However, be aware that the pervasive virtualization and automation which help define clouds also introduce new wrinkles for audit and other aspects of governance relative to an environment in which applications run on a known physical server.

- Enable developers to utilize public cloud resources as appropriate, but with an eye to having consistent development tools and platform environment on-premise and in the cloud. Cloud-based application development and test strategies should take into account the complete application lifecycle, including production deployment.

- You can start small with a proof-of-concept or a pilot project. However, implementing a cloud architecture is best approached as a strategic project that leverages existing IT resources and that provides maximum flexibility going forward.

The Platform

As we've covered in various contexts, enabling new applications to be written and deployed more quickly is no small part of cloud computing. However, most of what we've discussed so far relates to doing so at the infrastructure layer whether on-premise or in a public cloud. The reality, though, is that many application developers have no need or desire to work at this low level. Hence, there's a lot of developing interest in Platform-as-a-Service which explicitly provides abstractions and tools aimed at making developers more productive.

The rise of the hybrid platform

The Platform-as-a-Service moniker covers a lot of ground. At its broadest, it's almost a generic term for Web APIs. At its narrowest, it means a set of programmatic interfaces into a specific hosted application—essentially a way to extend Software-as-a-Service. However, for our purposes here, think of Platform-as-a-Service as an abstraction that lets developers focus on writing, running, and managing applications without having to unduly concern themselves with low-level plumbing such as provisioning and tuning operating system images.

Such a PaaS is an application platform comprised of an operating system, middleware and other software allowing applications to run on the cloud with much of the management, security, scaling and other stack related headaches abstracted away. The PaaS deals with system administration details like setting up servers or virtual machines, installing libraries or frameworks, configuring testing tools, and so forth. Ideally, the workflow for on-boarding an application should be as simple as pushing application code from a standard development environment on a PC using a version control system like Git, then going to an application's Web address to see the changes live.

In a later chapter, I'll peel back the abstraction and get into how it works. For now though, suffice it to say that it's a means to make developers more productive by letting them focus on developing rather than becoming mired in the requisite infrastructure.

Given that context, it's not surprising that most initial Platform-as-a-Service offerings were hosted services. After all, a hosted service is almost always going to serve as an easier and preferred on-ramp for developers who don't want to worry about operational details. That's certainly been our experience at Red Hat with our OpenShift Online Platform-as-a-Service offering, which makes deploying an application as easy as pushing it to a code repository. A PaaS like OpenShift Online handles details like auto-scaling, self-service, and monitoring applications—leaving developers to focus on creating applications with familiar tools, languages, and frameworks.

However, a hosted service is, as the name implies, hosted by someone else. And, for many organizations, that loss of control isn't acceptable, at least not for all of their applications. Using a PaaS that makes use of standard languages and development frameworks helps to a degree; once developed in that manner, an application can be deployed in any environment provisioned with appropriate operating system or middleware runtimes.

But because such a transplanted application loses access to the operational automation of a PaaS platform, a hosted service may still not be seen as ideal. As a result, the best alternative for many enterprises will be a hybrid PaaS approach, which allows organizations to gain the advantages of a PaaS while operating it in the manner of their choosing—whether hosted, on-premise, or a combination of the two.

As we'll see, in Red Hat's case, OpenShift Enterprise provides an on-premise counterpart to a hosted service. This makes it easier for system admins and enterprise developers to meet the needs of their developers, even when some or all of that development has to take place on infrastructure which the IT department directly controls.

The Synthesized Cloud: Hybrid Service Models by James Labocki

As a Technical Product Marketing Manager in Red Hat's Cloud Business Unit, James Labocki enables Red Hat's Solution Architects and Red Hat Consulting teams to understand Red Hat's technical cloud strategy. In doing so he defines the strategy for Red Hat CloudForms, an open hybrid cloud-management framework. James brings a unique perspective based on his experience as a customer, a consultant, and now a vendor of open source solutions. Previously, James helped customers realize the benefits of open source in their next generation architectures as Cloud and Virtualization Architect within Red Hat's Government Team. The following is adapted from a November 2012 blog post.

Website: www.allthingsopen.com

Twitter: @jameslabocki

Often, when speaking with organizations about a cloud opportunity I find myself asking questions to find out the appropriate service model, such as Infrastructure-as-a-Service (IaaS) or Platform-as-a-Service (PaaS) for the customer.

"Do you want to just bring your code?"

"Would you like to access the operating system and perform optimizations?"

"How do you feel about kernel semaphores?"

OK, maybe not that last one, but you get the idea. The answers to these questions often help me determine which one of the models, and thereby solutions, to recommend for the situation.

The Synthesized Cloud

Taking a step back, what is the purpose of having separate and distinct cloud computing models? Why couldn't the models be combined to allow organizations to use elements of each based on their needs?

One of the benefits of cloud computing is that it allows organizations to standardize while increasing reuse of software components. Given this, it should be a goal to provide organizations with the ability to use not just a hybrid cloud, but a hybrid service model—one in which elements of IaaS can be combined with elements of a PaaS. By realizing a synthesis of IaaS and PaaS service models, organizations can leverage the benefits of cloud computing more widely and realize its benefits even in what are often considered legacy, or traditional applications. Cloud Efficiencies Everywhere is, after all, a goal of Red Hat's Open Hybrid Cloud. I'll refer to this combining of IaaS and PaaS into a single service model as the synthesized cloud and I believe it is critical to realizing the full potential of cloud computing.

Why not just use PaaS?

Most organizations I have met with are extremely interested in PaaS. They find the increase in developer productivity PaaS can offer very attractive and the idea of "moving the chalk line" up to have developers bringing code instead of hardware descriptions as very exciting. PaaS is great, no doubt about it, but while PaaS can accelerate delivery for "Systems of Engagement," it often does not account for systems of record and other core business systems. There is evidence that supports the idea that organizations are shifting from systems of record to system of engagement, but this is not a shift that will happen overnight and, in some cases, systems of record will be maintained alongside or complemented by systems of engagement.

Beyond systems of record, there are technologies that exist at the infrastructure layer that can be exposed to the platform layer that might not yet be available in a PaaS (think data analytics and computing grid platforms such as Hadoop, Condor, etc). In time, some of these technologies might be moved into the PaaS layer, but we likely continue to see innovation happening at both the infrastructure and platform services model layers. In short, IaaS finds its fit in both building new applications that require specific understanding of the underlying infrastructure (networks, storage, etc) and as the foundation for hosting a PaaS. Consequently, the infrastructure services layer will always be important in organizations.

For these reasons, our service model must remain open and flexible while simultaneously having a single way to describe and manage both abstraction levels.

Use the Correct Mix

The ability to use both platform and infrastructure elements is critical to maintaining flexibility and evolving to an optimized IT infrastructure. Red Hat is well positioned to deliver the synthesis of Infrastructure and Platform service models. This has as much to do with the great engineering work and strategic decisions being made by Red Hat engineers as it does the open source model's propensity to drive modular design.

Some points to consider:

OpenShift Enterprise, Red Hat's PaaS, runs on Infrastructure (specifically, Red Hat Enterprise Linux).

Thousands of other applications run on Red Hat Enterprise Linux (RHEL).

Application Blueprints provide sustainable, reusable descriptions of any software running on Red Hat Enterprise Linux.

Red Hat CloudForms can deploy Application Blueprints to a number of underlying resource providers.

Because Application Blueprints can deploy any software running on RHEL and OpenShift Enterprise is software running on RHEL, we can deploy a Platform as a Service alongside traditional applications running on RHEL.

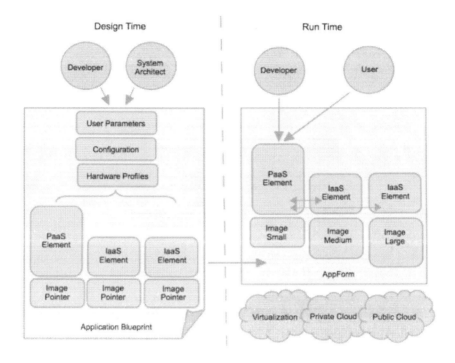

Figure 1 depicts the use of an Application Blueprint to deliver a hybrid service model of IaaS and PaaS. At design time, a developer and a system architect work together to design the Application Blueprint. This involves using CloudForms to define and build all the necessary images that will serve as the foundations for each element in the AppForm (a running Application Blueprint). CloudForms allows the system architect and developer to build all these images with the push of a button and tracks all the images at each provider. In this case, a single PaaS element and two IaaS elements were described in the Application Blueprint.

The design process also allows the system architect and developer to associate hardware profiles to each of the images, and specify how the software that runs on the images should be configured upon launch. Finally, user parameters can be accepted in the Application Blueprint, to allow for customization when the Application Blueprint is launched by it's intended end user. The result of designing an Application Blueprint is a customizable reusable and portable description of a complete application environment.

Once the Application Blueprint is designed and published to a catalog, users or developers are able to launch the Application Blueprint, the result of which is an AppForm at runtime. The running AppForm can contain both a PaaS and a mix of IaaS elements and CloudForms will orchestrate the configuration of the two service models together upon launch according to the design of the Application Blueprint.

An Example

Imagine an organization has a legacy human resources system of record. It's a client-server model[46] built on an Oracle relational database. Over time, they'd like to morph this system into a system that is more engaging for their employees. They'd also like to begin providing some data analysis to select individuals in the human resources department. In this case, replacing the system of record with a completely new system of engagement is not an option. This may be because of the cost associated with a rewrite or the fact that there are many back end processes that tie into the Oracle database that cannot be easily changed.

In this example, the Application Blueprint is designed to include an OpenShift PaaS which delivers a scalable, managed application platform (Tomcat in this case) and both an Oracle database and Hadoop. Once the Application Blueprint is launched users or developers can access this entire environment and begin working. This goes beyond gaining increased developer efficiency at just the platform layer—it drives many of the efficiencies of PaaS across the infrastructure as well.

---

[46] Client-server describes a specific application architecture in which part of the application runs in a datacenter (the server) and part of the application runs on a traditional PC (the client). For our purposes here, though, just think of it as a traditional enterprise application that's hard to use and hard to change.

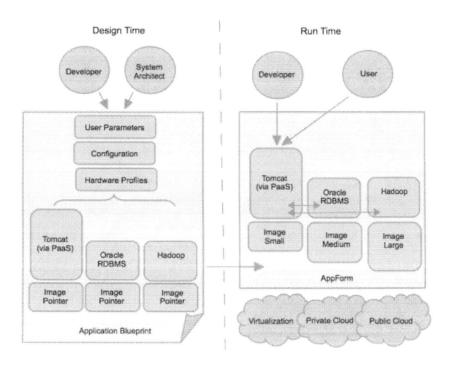

Further Benefits of a Hybrid Service Model

There are many other benefits to this synthesis of PaaS and IaaS
service models. One other I'd like to explore is its effect on system
testing. With a hybrid service model, not only do developers have
access to all the qualities of both PaaS and IaaS in a single description
that is portable, but the Application Lifecycle Environment framework
contained within CloudForms, along with its ability to automatically
provision both PaaS and IaaS, can be leveraged to lay the foundation
for a governed DevOps model.[47] This provides greater efficiency in
testing, accelerating delivery of applications, while allowing for

---

[47] DevOps refers to a melding of traditionally separate roles—the application
developer and the system operator. It's arguably sort of a trendy term but it does
point to a general breaking down on the walls between traditionally rather isolated
functions.

control over important aspects of both the Infrastructure and Platform layers.

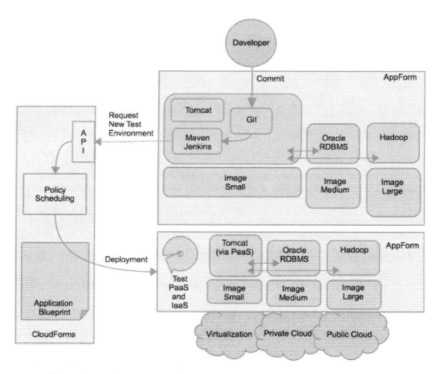

Figure 3 illustrates how the hybrid service model allows for a governed DevOps model to be implemented. Before the hybrid service model, developers needed to request the required IaaS elements in order to complete a system test. This process is often manual and time consuming. With a hybrid service model in place, upon commit of new code to the source control system, the continuous integration systems contained within the PaaS layer can request a new test environment be created that includes the required IaaS elements for system testing. This greatly reduces the time required to test, and in turn, accelerates application delivery.

Streamlining application development with PaaS

A lot of the attention around "cloud applications" focuses on Software-as-a-Service, which is to say complete applications delivered directly to the users of those applications. And SaaS is indeed an important cloud story. Whether we're talking about consumers and smaller businesses gaining access to applications they didn't have the resources or skills to run in-house in the past or whether we're talking about largely undifferentiated apps like email, SaaS can do away with the need for a lot of routine IT.

However, the infiltration of technology into more and more types of businesses—even ones that we didn't historically think of as especially dependent on information or computing, such as agriculture—has also fueled a huge appetite for custom applications. In fact, arguably the only thing staunching that appetite is the money and time it takes to develop applications. And that's what makes PaaS so interesting given how it's so focused on increasing developer productivity. Such productivity has a direct relationship to how quickly businesses can bring new services and products online—and how quickly they can start making money for the organization.

Some of this productivity increase comes from faster access to resources; no waiting for IT to order servers, provision them, and provide access. But that's really a benefit of cloud computing more broadly—whether a public cloud or a properly planned private one. The big benefit of PaaS specifically is that it lets developers focus on the things that matter for application development and ignore the things that don't. This means designing compelling user interfaces and appropriate database architectures, not configuring firewall settings or tuning operating system resource limits.

The benefits of PaaS aren't just limited to developers though. As an industry, we're seeing a shift away from strictly segregated operations and developer roles. The term "DevOps" was coined to capture this idea that application development increasingly embeds operational concepts such as availability and scaling. In part, this is the result of architectures which deal with these concepts at the application, rather than the underlying infrastructure, layer.

PaaS is a great match for a DevOps model because the PaaS itself can help provide auto-scaling, self-service, standard pre-configured services, and other features which historically would have been considered part of IT operations. Under a hosted model, these capabilities are all provided directly to the developer and the underlying plumbing—adding server resources as needed, remediating infrastructure failures, monitoring for security issues—is handled by the service provider. With an on-premise PaaS, on the other hand, IT operations controls (and is responsible for) the infrastructure but can choose to pass a degree of that control over to the developers. PaaS can therefore be a win for admins as well as developers by providing a framework and tools for delegating responsibilities while retaining overall control of policy.

Many organizations see PaaS as an opportunity to standardize development workflows—leading to increased consistency and productivity. Standardization within a given organization can only become more important as the number and scale of applications increase and as more organizations move to more agile development models and more rapid, incremental updates to production systems.

The tremendous excitement around PaaS can be seen both through the growing adoption within the developer community, and the number of vendors entering the space with both online and on-premise PaaS solutions. Although initially used primarily by early adopters & innovators—including individual developers, startups, and small companies—PaaS is entering the mainstream.

What is enabling this mainstream adoption by larger enterprises and a broader section of the market?

One change is that PaaS is becoming more multi-lingual. Red Hat has conducted surveys at several events; the results consistently show that most respondents intend to develop software for cloud environments using a similar mix of languages to those they're using today. PaaS platforms which limit developers to a specific language on a specific hosting platform have often been criticized by developers because they constrain this choice. It's telling that a number of language- and framework-specific PaaSes have shifted toward a more polyglot (multiple languages/frameworks) approach.

Red Hat OpenShift, for example, has the concept of "cartridges," which are the mechanism through which platform services are exposed. In the initial on-premise offering, there are cartridges for Java, PHP, Ruby, Perl, and Python as well as, for data services, MySQL and Postgres. It also has community-supported node.js and MongoDB flavors.

Another important consideration is the support for different operational models. An online service serves as a simple on-ramp for a developer who just wants to try out a service. Certain new-style Internet businesses will even be comfortable with using an online service for all their production applications—especially if, as in the case of OpenShift, their code can be moved elsewhere without making changes.

However, many organizations still prefer or require that at least a subset of their applications run in an environment over which they have full control. They want the operational benefits of PaaS but they want to be in charge of the infrastructure. They may also prefer to expose fewer options to developers than is typically the case under a DevOps model. Arguably, this more traditional "ITOps" philosophy will morph into more functionally integrated organizational structures over time. Nonetheless, such changes will happen incrementally and, therefore, PaaS offerings that can support a variety of operational philosophies have significant benefits.

A PaaS architectural example: OpenShift

OpenShift Enterprise is a commercial product, offered through a subscription like other Red Hat open source products, that lets IT organizations set up and manage their own PaaS. As with all other Red Hat subscription offerings, OpenShift Enterprise takes the open source code that Red Hat donated to the OpenShift Origin project (under the Apache 2.0 license) and makes it into a reliable and supported product for enterprise use.

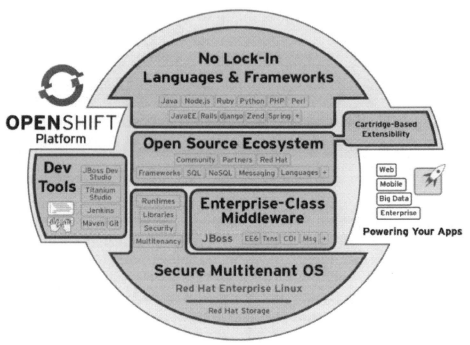

Architecturally, the only dependency for OpenShift Enterprise is Red Hat Enterprise Linux (RHEL). OpenShift Enterprise can run on a bare metal system running RHEL. It can run on virtual infrastructure provided by Red Hat Enterprise Virtualization or another virtualization platform. The RHEL infrastructure can be managed and provisioned using tools such as Red Hat CloudForms or Red Hat Network Satellite. But OpenShift Enterprise is a PaaS orchestration layer that is independent of any specific tooling or infrastructure (other than RHEL).

OpenShift Enterprise runs in one instance of RHEL (the "broker")[48] which manages one or more other instances of RHEL (the "nodes"). OpenShift Enterprise then provides the mechanisms for multiple applications to run within those nodes securely and with predictable performance, as well as providing monitoring and auto-scaling capabilities for those applications.

Application multi-tenancy, whereby multiple applications (each consisting of one or more "gears") can co-exist within each node, is provided through a variety of RHEL features and managed by the OpenShift Enterprise broker. These RHEL features include:

- SELinux, an implementation of a mandatory access control (MAC) mechanism in the Linux kernel, checks for allowed operations at a level beyond what standard discretionary access controls (DAC) can provide. It was initially created by the US National Security Agency and can enforce rules on files and processes in a Linux system, and on their actions, based on defined policy. SELinux provides a high level of isolation between applications running within OpenShift Enterprise.

- Control Groups (Cgroups) offer a powerful way to allocate processor, memory, and I/O resources among applications. They provide fine-grained control of resource utilization in terms of memory consumption, IO (storage and networking) utilization and process priority—enabling the establishment of policies that provide quality-of-service guarantees.

- Kernel namespaces separate groups of processes so that they cannot "see" resources in other groups. Thus, from the perspective of an application running in OpenShift, it has access to a complete running RHEL system even though, in reality, it may be one of many applications running within a single instance of RHEL.

Collectively, these technologies implement an approach that is similar in certain respects to what are sometimes called "containers," but with greater isolation and minimal resource overhead. The philosophy behind OpenShift was informed by its genesis as an online service,

---

[48] Multiple instances of the broker can be deployed as a high availability cluster for redundancy purposes.

now called OpenShift Online, in which high security and high efficiency are both paramount.

Auto-scaling, which is built into the OpenShift Online service, is also available in the on-premise OpenShift Enterprise. When you deploy an application through OpenShift, you can deploy it with scaling either enabled or disabled. If you deploy your application with scaling disabled, what you deploy is what you'll have, whether it's in one gear or several.

If you deploy with auto-scaling enabled, then the application can scale up and consume additional gears based on the usage of that application and its needs for more resources. For example, instead of, say, putting a MySQL Database and JBoss EAP Enterprise Middleware into one gear, you would put MySQL into a separate gear, put JBoss EAP in its own gear, and then set up a software-based load balancer, which such as HAProxy, as a third gear. HAProxy would then detect the level of requests coming to the application. If it sees traffic exceeding a certain threshold, it will make a request to the broker to spin up an additional JBoss EAP gear and configure it using JBoss clustering techniques.

In addition to a variety of programming languages and frameworks— including the latest Java EE 6 technologies—OpenShift also supports popular development tools. One such tool is Apache Maven, a software project management tool. Maven can manage a project's build, reporting, and documentation from a central model. Another is Jenkins, which is often used as a continuous integration system, making it easier for developers to integrate changes to the project, and making it easier for users to obtain a fresh build—thereby increasing productivity. LDAP directory service and Kerberos network authentication protocol plug-ins let IT integrate OpenShift PaaS into their enterprise authentication systems so that when developers come to OpenShift they can authenticate with their LDAP and/or Kerberos credentials.

OpenShift Enterprise's architectural approach has big benefits for developers and their organizations. It's built on a proven secure multi-tenant operating system, Red Hat Enterprise Linux, but provides maximum flexibility in how that operating system is deployed and managed. It provides support for tools and languages that are both powerful and familiar. And it gives a great deal of control to administrators while making the move from being a RHEL administrator to a PaaS administrator as seamless as possible with default policies and settings which satisfy many requirements right out of the box.

Multi-tenancy in PaaS with Matt Hicks

Adapted from a June 2012 interview with Red Hat Principal Engineer Matt Hicks who discusses what's needed to provide security and predictable performance in a Platform-as-a-Service environment in which traditional infrastructure techniques to isolate applications, such as using separate operating system instances, aren't always appropriate.

Matt Hicks is one of the founding members of the Red Hat OpenShift team. He has spent over a decade in software engineering with a variety of roles in development, operations, architecture, and management. His real expertise is in bridging the gap between developing code and actually running it in production.

Website: http://mattoncloud.org/

Twitter: @matthicksj

Multi-tenancy; it's a tough term because it's fairly abstract. When we talk about multi-tenancy, it's good to frame it. My definition would be being able to run multiple workloads on the same instance of an operating system. That operating system might be a virtual instance, it might be a bare-metal instance. Multi-tenancy means that when you run these workloads, they're segmented from each other, they're secure, they can't access each other's data, they can't access the other processes, and they each have somewhat of a feeling that they own the entire machine.

We know using the operating system to provide segmentation really well. Virtual machines are an important layer that does this, a great means of providing essentially separate operating systems on a single physical server.

The challenge with VMs is, especially in the PaaS space is that our density requirements, the amount of stuff that you have to run, is extremely high, and the cost pressure to get your costs low is very intense as well. A virtual machine carries a lot of operational costs for doing that segmentation. You have sysadmins that are putting up firewall rules and putting them in separate networks, and they have to be patched and updated. If you run a workload per VM, it's very secure, it's very well segmented, but it'll probably be very expensive in a PaaS model.

When we look at multi-tenancy, one of the things that worries me about multi-tenancy is the people that just run traditional, Unix-style segmentation. They take a VM, they run a bunch of processes on it, and then they basically pray that permissions and everything are set right and there is security between them. That's what we tend to call discretionary access control; you'll see the acronym, DAC.

Discretionary access control requires that you're essentially perfect. You have all the permissions right. You have all the users properly segmented. The machine is always patched. There are no backdoors for somebody to get from one app to the other.

I think that's very risky. We see a lot of that in the market. That's what people are doing for multi-tenancy. I think that's a security problem just waiting to happen.

Luckily there's a very industry-standard way of solving this. That's moving from discretionary access control to mandatory access control with SELinux. The power of doing that is that it's like moving from a blacklist model, where you have to say all the things that aren't allowed. SELinux moves stuff to more of a whitelist model, where you list the things that are allowed on those machines, and it brings with it a tremendous amount of security in a multi-tenant space.

In PaaS, we know what applications are doing. It's a very effective thing for us to be able to list the actions that they should take and then block everything else. I think, with SELinux, there's a ton of security and segmentation ability with normal multi-tenancy. You can get the best of both worlds there.

Organizations like the National Security Agency have been involved in the development of SELinux, so some pretty high-security people have had a big hand in this. It's becoming best practice across the board. Even if you're using virtualization, you want your hypervisors controlled by SELinux because it is that good at helping to avoid exploits. Combining that with the power of being able to segment Unix processes, it's a great combination. You get the density benefits of avoiding VM sprawl. You have a smaller list of VMs that you have to carry that operational cost of updating and maintaining them on, and you can carry a wide variety of workloads within those VMs and get a tremendous amount of segmentation between them just with SELinux. It's not new; it's really leveraging the capabilities that are already in the Linux operating system.

In the Platform-as-a-Service space, we're really seeing multi-tenancy as sort of an evolving standard in that space. The way it's achieved is very different, but the major players, from Google to Heroku to VMware's CloudFoundry, are all using process segmentation, to one degree or another, to achieve the density that's required in PaaS. I think what we'll see going forward is, when you're in the PaaS space, the demands of being able to segment based on multi-tenancy are going to be the standard. I think that the techniques right now are different across the board. Some people fork the frameworks themselves to take out the insecure things. Some people are just using technologies like LXC with nothing else. Our view is we use basically every tool in the toolkit plus SELinux to be able to have the most secure option. I think that will still evolve a little bit, but I think it's pretty safe to say that multi-tenancy in this space is probably here to stay.

In the PaaS space users interact with components of the operating system, but it's pretty well accepted that you don't have control of the full machine. You might need to get access to ports, but you don't have every port on the system. You might need to get access to HTTP routing, but you don't own the actual top-level Apache Web server instance. I think that's been pretty well established in the market. That benefit of limiting the use case lets us make multi-tenancy much more powerful. If we didn't have any limits, we'd have to give each user their own virtual machine because they would expect to be able to control everything on it.

Virtual machines have a great role in being able to provide segmentation. But all of the traditional hosting techniques that were used 20 years ago to segment stuff are still being used by us today, plus this newer generation of tooling, like Linux control groups and SELinux and kernel namespaces. You don't have full control of the machine, like they would in a VM, but it helps us strike the balance a little bit better and lets users have a lot of ability even though they're in this sandbox on the machine.

One of the things I love about PaaS is the demands of things like density are really driving this resurgence in tools that have been around, in some cases, for a couple of decades. I think it's an exciting space to see the combination of those tools with newer technologies being brought together. It makes that spectrum a lot more powerful, whether physical hardware is what you need for your use case, or whether you can do it with purely virtual machines, or whether you have the need to start packing density in controlled use cases and go more down the containers and SELinux-type model. It's great. I have more fun with Linux these days than in a long time.

Will the cloud change programming?

There are hundreds of programming languages—perhaps thousands if experimental and academic variants are included. That said, the number of widely used languages is much smaller, numbering perhaps in the dozens, with fewer still broadly relevant to general-purpose server operations and Web software.

In fact, what's so notable about the computer programming language landscape over time isn't so much its diversity and adaptability, but rather its inertia. COBOL and Fortran, the longtime standards for business and scientific programming respectively, remain in use—albeit less widely so than at one time. Object-oriented programming, which bundles data together with the associated functions that operate on that data for more structured and maintainable code, came into initial widespread use largely through extending an existing language, C. (Although the practice was embedded in many other languages over time.) C itself, originally designed as a language for programming systems at a very low level, was put into use for all sorts of application programming tasks for which it was arguably not very well-suited.

Does this change with cloud computing or, to be more precise, with an increased emphasis on browser-centric application access, big and unstructured data processing, and the development of a huge mobile ecosystem?

To some degree, it already has. Scripting languages, including JavaScript but also Perl, Python, PHP, Ruby, and others are children of the Web. Languages such as these, which lend themselves to writing code quickly with less of the stringent correctness checking common to traditional enterprise code-writing, have become the norm in many Web environments.

But, so far, cloud computing hasn't sparked much change beyond what the Web already did. When Red Hat conducted a survey among US VMworld (virtualization giant VMware's user show) attendees in 2011, we asked about the primary language and framework for software development that respondents use today and that they plan to use in the cloud. Java EE and Microsoft .NET led the results with about 30 percent each with most of the other responses divided among Web-oriented languages like Perl, Python, and PHP. Not really a surprise given the enterprise-y and somewhat Windows-centric orientation of VMworld, which isn't exactly an open source development hotspot. What struck me as more interesting was that the "use today" and the "planning to use in the cloud" questions tallied up to essentially identical results. At least this audience seems to have a strong bias towards portably bringing their current development tools into cloud-based environments.

Of these results, Al Gillen, program vice president for system software at market researcher IDC, said that he "thought it very revealing that yesterday's frameworks were target for tomorrow's apps." He went on to write that "tools will evolve and utilize new programming frameworks, then use will evolve over time, not so revolutionary."

Nor have the more radical approaches to dealing with large-scale parallel operations on the server side taken off in a big way. We've mostly seen a combination of incrementalism and the adoption of specific tools and libraries, such as MapReduce, which target specific important types of problems such as looking for patterns in large data sets.

Hosted platform-as-a-service clouds introduce new possibilities to broaden the Web programming landscape. However, to the degree that an application programming interface (API) is limited to a single provider, moving an application elsewhere will require at least some porting. As a result, while we do see some providers offering APIs that are specific to a hosted environment, there's a strong argument for the flexibility of application portability across on-premise and a variety of hosted clouds.

The overall picture I see is one of change, but change that is mostly evolutionary and that doesn't involve a radical overnight shift away from existing models.

The developer landgrad - Another way to look at DevOps by Coté

Michael Coté works on cloud strategy at Dell. He wrote this 2011 blog post while an analyst at RedMonk. Previous to RedMonk, he was a developer at BMC Software at the Austin campus. His primary work was developing the BMC Performance Manager (née PATROLExpress), a web application for network and Web site monitoring.

Website: http://drunkandretired.com

Twitter: @cote

Developers are Insourcing

Developers have been in-sourcing tasks they'd previously jettisoned from their core functionality for a few years now and cloud computing has brought one more land-grab: operations. Agile tricked developers into caring about QA and testing, but also requirements and product management. Now, DevOps is "tricking" developers to care about operations. I put tricking in quotes because the developers actually want this—the good ones at least. The benefits, or at least goals, are clear: delivering software that users like with a more frequent cadence. Those are the two aspects of software development that most interest me now: frequent functionality and using rapid feedback-loops to improve the user experience and overall usefulness of the software.

A Brief, Hand-wavy History

At the very beginning, development teams did everything, or at the very least were intimately involved: gathered requirements, writing the code, testing the code, running the code. IT being expensive, organizations sought to divide up those tasks into shared resources, often under different management chains. Developers, of course, also just wanted to write code: not "talk with customers about what they needed" (requirements and product management) or keep their applications humming along nicely in production (operations).

Throw in mainframe MIPs accounting and high costs, and you can see how separating out those rascally developers from expensive mainframe toys makes business sense, at least in a spreadsheet. (Side-note: with the metered pricing of cloud computing, thus far there's no reason to think that in 10 or so years, cloud computing resources will be any less iron-gripped controlled than mainframe resources–that is, use and consumption of them will be slowed down in favor of controlling costs. We'll see.)

And writing and running tests? What developer wants to do that?

Agile Starts to In-source: QA[49]

One of the emergent principles of Agile (perhaps an anti-pattern) is that once the core team who wrote the software gives control of that software to another group, overall quality tends to go down. This isn't across the board, but you tend to see that. As an individual, if you don't somehow "own" the software, you won't give it the same love and care that an "owner" will. This applies to QA and operations, usually not so much to product management.

Agile is always trying to get developers to do more process. To own more of the software lifecycle. It never says this outright, but cynical developers will spot it right away: "wait, my job is to write code, not write-up use cases and rank them. Let alone help take care of my software in production, in the hands of dirty users. I mean: are you going to pay me more?"

Somehow, Agile got developers to care about QA. It started small with unit testing by promising, after a huge amount of initial work, to make them more productive. Then functional tests came in, and now if you've got yourself wired up correctly, you can test whole use cases (or "stories" to use the term Agile hid the dread "use case" behind).

---

[49] Quality Assurance, i.e. the organization or function that tests code.

The bigger win was getting QA to be part of the development team. In reality, good QA people are often the foremost experts on the product —they're the ones that spend hours, weeks poking and prodding it. Getting their input, starting at the beginning, is a great way to improve software. As with developers who are writing and running tests, the QA person ceases to be "just QA": they're one of the many owners of the software.

"I take the requirements from the customer to the developers."

Seeking feedback and rich interaction with users hasn't always been a strong-point of developers. They haven't wanted to do product management (in this context: figuring out what users/customers want and then prioritizing which ones get into which release). "That's someone else's job" is what you'd hear. As with QA, that role has seeped a bit into developers hands as well. There's simply not enough time in the day to write code, test, and also do product management, so it's probably a good idea to have a whole person filling that role: but, having that person be the sole conduit between developers and users is not entirely helpful.

Thanks to the ability to run software as a service (SaaS) and mature cloud offerings, a lot of the feedback teams need to do product management can now be automated. If you're running your application as a SaaS, you can see what every single user is doing all the time. It's like you have infinite one-way mirror usability tests going on. Public web apps (Amazon, Facebook, etc.) have known this for a long time, getting into advanced practices like A/B feature testing: let's release two different ways of implementing this feature to sub-sets of users and see which one results in more book sales, and then we'll switch everyone over the better one. What you're driving at is feeding aggregated user behavior data into the product management process.

There's a quote I use all the time from Alterity's Brian Sweat that I use all the time to summarize this point:

I can actually look at [a feature] and say, 'nobody uses feature X.' It's not even being looked at. And it really helps us shape the future of the app which, on a desktop product, we don't have a lot of data like that.

There's two concepts running around here that I speak a lot about: frequent functionality and rapid feedback loops. Getting features in small chunks in production sooner and then collecting a huge amount of usage feedback from users. You're first delighting your users by keeping your software up-to-date and more functional (a lesson learned from the consumer space where new frequent functionality and integrations with other services is key for long-term success) and also giving yourself the chance to see what works best (or worst!) with users. You can empirically improve the quality of your software. And here, by "quality" I don't mean "bug free" (which is a less helpful definition in this context) but something more like "the ability to help users do their job better, faster, and more profitably."

Operations

Ask any developer if they'd like to take a pager and be woken up at 3am to reboot a server. You can guess what the answer is. A blank stare that says "no" in a string of four-letter words. These guys are coders, not pager monkeys.

And yet, developers are increasingly taking on that task, even if perhaps not letting those bat-belt ops guys clip a pager onto the developer's t-shirt. The speed at which cloud computing technologies and practices allow developers to get their core job done (spinning up virtual labs, getting access to resources without having to wait 6 weeks for the DBA to create a new column in a table, etc.) has sold developers on cloud computing. Throw in SaaS-ified parts of the development tool-chain like GitHub, and you start to see why developers like cloud-based technology so much: it speeds up their work, gives them more power (they don't have to ask IT permission for a server, and then wait for it), and overall improves their ability to produce good software.

As developers using cloud computing technologies get closer and closer to production, you can see them starting to in-source even operations. At the bleeding edge, those using Platform-as-a-Services (PaaS) are almost forced into doing this. Indeed, as its name implies, much of DevOps is about bringing the operations function back to the core team.

This doesn't suggest that you get rid of the operations people—the good ones at least. Rather, it means that, as with QA and product management, their role moves from "keeping the lights green" to "delivering good, productive experiences." Operations becomes one of the product owners, not just the "monkeys" who hook up wires to servers and increase disk-space.

As some point, IT became a cost-center, a provider of "services" to the business. That's terrible for them. No one wants to be the manager of a "shared resource." Just go ask your janitorial staff or the guy who keeps your office supply closet stocked how secure and well paid they are. Before the current crop of IT Management technologies finally ripened (Agile development, virtualization, open source, and now cloud), perhaps, taking this "services" approach was cost effective. But, now it means that IT has one way to show value to the rest of the company: budget cuts. For IT, the promise is to become top-line revenue: part of the way a company makes money, not hidden somewhere in the expenses.

(Hey, I'm a big IT Management guy here, so realize that I'm being tongue-in-check with this whole "monkey" thing. If you want equal servings the other way: "Developers? Those are the guys who write bugs, right?")

Automation

All of this in-sourcing relies on automating parts of what's being brought back to the core development team: automating testing with the right testing frameworks and continuous integration tools, automating understanding how users are interacting with your software with cloud-driven feedback, and automating IT management in production.

Evaluating Offerings & Programs

To me, this understanding that automation is key is critical because it means what I've been seeing here and there is driven by actual, new technology: not just vapor-ware and Unicorn-meat. It means something else great: if someone comes peddling DevOps or some other wacky cloud-based way to improve your software delivery process, you can ask them to show you the tools—" where's the beef?" and all that.

Avoiding Outsourcing

> [I]f you worked for AT&T in my day, it was a great bureaucracy. Who in the hell was really thinking about the shareholder or anything else? And in a bureaucracy, you think the work is done when it goes out of your in-basket into somebody else's in-basket. But, of course, it isn't. It's not done until AT&T delivers what it's supposed to deliver. So you get big, fat, dumb, unmotivated bureaucracies.
>
> –Charles Munger

There's a tremendous amount of "cultural change" (read: getting employees to do things differently and like it) needed, but the hope is that this trend of developers in-sourcing tasks means that cultural change will be possible. It doesn't happen often, but many parts of the IT department (developers, QA, and a bit of ops) are actually looking for new ways of doing things. The best part is that the promise—that some folks have been realizing—is that IT can become part of the business, not just a cut-to-the-bone cost center that keeps email up and running and AntiVirus software updated.

Or, to put it all more simply: Conway's Law.[50]

---

[50] An adage named after computer programmer Melvin Conway stating that "organizations that design systems ... are constrained to produce designs which are copies of the communication structures of these organizations."

The golden age of enterprise apps: Why PaaS matters

When the notice for a panel about enterprise PaaS I would be appearing on went live a while ago, it attracted the attention of an anonymous commenter. The tone of the comment was about what you'd expect from an anon—which is to say of a tenor that could result in rather unpleasant repercussions if delivered in person. But, that aside, the substance of the remark is worth considering. To wit, is it true that, as this individual wrote, "PaaS for IT is complete 100% BS. All new applications are SaaS. Who is funding IT to build new applications?"

It's not a completely risible opinion. After all, we don't need to look far to see great examples of Software-as-a-Service replacing packaged on-premise applications which, in turn, had often replaced largely bespoke software sometime in the past. Certainly, it's unlikely any business would write a payroll or benefits application for its own use and few enough would sensibly tackle custom customer relationship management given the existence of Salesforce.com, SugarCRM, and others. Indeed, the idea that standardized functions can be largely commoditized is central to many cloud computing concepts more broadly. And, certainly, many organizations spend way too much time and money reinventing the wheel because they see themselves as a uniquely special little flower. (And they're mostly not.)

But to extrapolate from such examples to the death of application development is to take an unfounded leap.

For one thing, it misunderstands a platform such as Salesforce.com. Yes, Salesforce is a SaaS used by countless enterprise sales forces and marketing teams to track customer contacts, forecasts, and sales campaigns. But that's the view from the perspective of the end user. From the perspective of independent software vendors and enterprise developers, Salesforce is a platform that can be extended in many ways. Just to give you an idea of scale, Dreamforce—Salesforce's annual developer conference—had over 90,000 attendees in 2012.

That's a huge conference. Industry analyst Judith Hurwitz calls Force.com, the platform aspect of Salesforce, a "PaaS anchored to a SaaS environment."

Thus, even using a SaaS doesn't eliminate application development. In fact, it may enable and accelerate more of it by reducing or eliminating a lot of the undifferentiated heavy lifting and allowing companies to focus on customizations specific to their industry, products, or sales strategy.

Another analyst, Eric Knipp of Gartner, states the case for ongoing application development even more strongly. He writes that "While I don't debate that 'the business' will have more 'packages' to choose from (loosely referring to packages as both traditional deployed solutions and cloud-sourced SaaS), I also believe that enterprises will be developing more applications themselves than ever before." In fact, he goes so far as to call today "a golden age of enterprise application development."

The reason is that PaaS makes development faster, easier, and—ultimately—cheaper. But businesses don't have a fixed appetite for applications, which is to say business services that they can either sell or leverage to otherwise increase revenues or reduce costs. We're especially hearing a lot of talk around business analytics and "big data" today. Likewise for mobile. But, really, information and applications are increasingly central to more and more businesses, even ones that one didn't historically think of as especially high-tech or IT-heavy.

The companies that grew up on the Web have always had IT technology at their core. Nearly as well known are examples from companies that design and manufacture high technology components, or financial services firms which depend on the latest and greatest hardware and software to rapidly price and execute trades. These types of businesses are cutting edge on the "3rd Platform," as IDC calls it—but that's what we've come to expect in these industries. What's most different today is that the cutting edge IT story doesn't begin and end with such companies. Rather, it's nearly pervasive.

Media today is digital media. The vast server farms at animation studios such as Dreamworks are perhaps the most obvious example. And their computing needs have only grown as animation has gone 3D. But essentially all content is digitized in various forms. For example, sports clips are catalogued and indexed so that they can be retrieved at a moment's notice—whether for a highlights reel or a premium mobile offering (a huge monetization opportunity in any case).

How about laundry? Now, that's low tech. Yet Mac-Gray Corporation redefined laundry room management. It introduced LaundryView, which allows students/residents to monitor activity in their specific laundry rooms so they can see whether a machine is free or their laundry is done. It's been visited by 5 million people and the company has added on-line payment and service dispatch systems.

Agriculture is an industry that suggests pastoral images of tractors and rows of crops. Yet, seed producer Monsanto holds more than 15,000 patents for genetically-altered seeds and other inventions. (A category of intellectual property protection which may be controversial but a depth of IP which is no less striking for that.)

I could continue to offer examples both familiar and less so. However, the basic point is straightforward: increasingly, information technology isn't something important to a few industries and uses but is, rather, permeating just about everywhere. It's about creating new types of services, better connecting to customers, increasing efficiency, delivering better market intelligence, and creating better consumer experiences.

And that means businesses will need to leverage platforms that streamline their development processes and make it possible to more quickly and economically create the applications they need to be competitive. Will they leverage pure SaaS too? (And, for that matter, public cloud services such as those provided by the likes of Amazon and Rackspace?) Sure. The focus should be on differentiating where differentiating adds value, not spending time and resources on "me-too" plumbing.

But that's what PaaS is best at. Making it easier for developers to focus on applications, not infrastructure. Enterprise application development is a long way from dead. But maybe the old way of doing it is.

Cloud as the death of middleware? by Mark Little

Dr. Mark Little serves as the senior director of middleware engineering at Red Hat. Prior to taking over this role in 2008, Mark served as the SOA technical development manager and director of standards. Additionally, Mark was a distinguished engineer and chief architect and co-founder at Arjuna Technologies, a spin-off from HP. He has worked in the area of reliable distributed systems since the mid-80s with a PhD in fault-tolerant distributed systems, replication, and transactions.

Originally published February 13, 2010.

Website: http://markclittle.blogspot.com/

Twitter: @nmcl

Over the last few months I've been hearing and reading people suggesting that the Cloud ([fill in your own definition]) is either the death of middleware, or the death of "traditional" middleware. What this tells me is that those individuals don't understand the concepts behind middleware ("traditional" or not). In some ways that's not too hard to understand given the relatively loose way in which we use the term 'middleware'. Often within the industry middleware is something we all understand when we're talking about it, but it's not something that we tend to be able to identify clearly: what one person considers application may be another's middleware component. In my world, middleware is basically anything that exists above the operating system and below the application (I think the fact that these days we tend to ignore the old ISO 7 Layer stack[51] is a real shame because that can only help such a definition.)

---

[51] A family of information exchange standards developed starting in the late 1970s. Most of the actual protocols ended up little used, although the stack model has been widely referenced, primarily in computer networking discussions.

But anyway, middleware has existed in one form or another for decades. There are obvious examples of "it" including DCE, CORBA, JEE and .NET, but then some other not so obvious ones such as the Web: yes, the WWW is a middleware system, including most of the usual suspects such as naming, addressing, security, message passing etc. And yes, over the past few years I've heard people suggest that the Web is also the death of middleware. For the same reasons that Cloud isn't its death knell, neither was the Web: middleware is ubiquitous and all but the most basic applications need "it", where "it" can be a complete middleware infrastructure such as JEE or just some sub-components, such as security or transactions. Now this doesn't mean that what constitutes middleware for the Cloud is exactly what we've all been using over the past few years. That would be as crazy a suggestion as assuming CORBA was the ultimate evolution of middleware or that Web Services architecture would replace JEE or .NET (something which some people once believed). Middleware today is an evolution of middleware from the 1960s and I'm sure it will continue to evolve as the areas to which we apply it change and evolve. I think it is also inevitable that Cloud will evolve, as we decide precisely what it is that we want it to do (as well as what "it" is) based upon both positive and negative experiences of what's out there currently. (That's why we have the Web today, after all.)

Implementations such as Google App Engine are interesting toys at the moment, offering the ability to deploy relatively simple applications that may be based on cut-down APIs with which people are familiar in a non-Cloud environment. But I'm fairly sure that if you consider what constitutes middleware for the vast majority of applications, the offerings today are inadequate. Now maybe the aim is for people who require services such as security, transactions, etc. to reimplement them in such a way that they can be deployed on-demand to the types of Cloud infrastructures around today. If that is the case then it does seem to solve the problem (bare minimum capabilities available initially) but I take issue with that approach too: as an industry we simply cannot afford to revisit the (almost) NIH[52]

---

[52] Not Invented Here.

syndromes that have scarred the evolution of middleware and software engineering in general over the past four decades. For instance, when Java came on the scene there was a rush to reimplement security, messaging, transactions etc. in this new, cool language. The industry and its users spent many years revisiting concepts, capabilities, services etc. that existed elsewhere and often had done so reliably and efficiently for decades, just so we could add the "Java" badge to them. OK, some things really did need reimplementing and rethinking (recall what I said about evolution), but certainly not as much as was reworked. This is just one example though: if you look back at DCE, CORBA, COM/DCOM, .NET etc. you'll see it has happened before in a very Battlestar Galactica-like situation.

Therefore, if we have to reimplement all of the core capabilities that have been developed over the years (even just this century) then we are missing the point and it really will take us another decade to get to where we need to be. However, don't read into this that I believe that current middleware solutions are perfect today either for Cloud applications or non-Cloud applications. We've made mistakes. But we've also gotten more things right than wrong. Plus if you look at any enterprise middleware stack, whether from the 21st or 20th century, you'll see many core capabilities or services are common throughout. Cloud does not change that. In my book it's about building on what we've done so far, making it "Cloud aware" (whatever that turns out to mean), and leveraging existing infrastructural investments both in terms of hardware and software (and maybe even peopleware).

Of course there'll be new things that we'll need to add to the infrastructure for supporting Cloud applications, just as JEE doesn't match CORBA exactly, or CORBA doesn't match DCE, etc. There may be new frameworks and languages involved too. But this new Cloud wave (hmmm, mixing metaphors there I think) needs to build on what we've learned and developed rather than being an excuse to reimplement or remake the software world in "our" own image. That would be far too costly in time and effort, and I have yet to be convinced that it would result in anything substantially better than the alternative approach. If I were to try to sum up what I'm saying here it would be: Evolution Rather Than Revolution!

The Path Ahead

Much of this book has focused on cloud computing in the here and now with a certain big company user and big company computer infrastructure slant.

Think of cloud computing, in this sense, as being about trends in how complexes of computers are architected, how applications are written and loaded onto those systems and made to do useful work, how servers communicate with each other and with the outside world, and how administrators manage and provide access. This trend also encompasses all the infrastructure and "plumbing" that makes it possible to effectively coordinate data centers full of systems working as a unified compute resource as opposed to islands of specialized capacity.

Devices, data, and developers

Cloud computing, in the sense I've used it throughout this book, embodies all the big changes in back-end computation. Many of these are in some way the product of Moore's Law, Intel co-founder Gordon Moore's 1965 observation that the number of transistors it's economically possible to build into an integrated circuit doubles approximately every two years. This exponential increase in the density of the switches at the heart of all computer logic has led to corresponding increases in computational power—even if the specific ways that transistors get turned into performance have shifted over time.

Moore's Law has also had indirect consequences. Riding Moore's Law requires huge investments in both design and manufacturing. Intel's next-generation Fab 42 manufacturing facility in Arizona is expected to cost more than $5 billion to build and equip. Although not always directly related to Moore's Law, other areas of the computing "stack"— especially in hardware such as disk drives—require similarly outsized investments. The result has been an industry oriented around horizontal specialties such as chips, servers, disk drives, storage arrays, operating systems, and databases rather than, as was once the case, integrated systems designed and built by a single vendor.

This industry structure implies standardization with a relatively modest menu of mainstream choices within each level of the stack: x86 and perhaps ARM for server processors, Linux and Windows for operating systems, Ethernet and InfiniBand for networking, and so forth. This standardization, in concert with other technology trends such as virtualization, makes it possible to create large and highly automated pools of computing which can scale up and down with traffic, can be re-provisioned for new purposes rapidly, can route around failures of many types, and can provide streamlined self-service access for users. Open source has been a further important catalyst. Without open source, it's difficult to imagine that infrastructures on the scale of those at Google and Amazon would be possible.

In this final section, I widen my beam and consider some other intersecting and supporting trends, trends that indeed are often conflated with cloud computing

Mobility—the device if you would—is, in a sense, the flip side of the cloud. If cloud computing is the data center of the future, mobility is the client. Perhaps the most obvious shift here is away from "fat client" PC dominance and towards simpler client devices like tablets and smartphones connecting through wireless networks using Web browsers and lightweight app store applications. This sea change is increasingly changing how organizations think about providing their employees with computers, a shift that often goes by the "Bring Your Own Device" phrase.

However, there's much more to the broad mobility trend than just tablets and smartphones. The "Internet of Things," a term attributed to RFID pioneer Kevin Ashton, posits a world of ubiquitous sensors that can be used to make large systems, such as the electric grid or a city's traffic patterns, "smarter." Which is to say, able to make adjustments for efficiency or other reasons in response to changes in the environment. While this concept has long had a certain just-over-the-horizon futurist aspect, more and more devices are getting plugged into the Internet, even if the changes are sufficiently gradual that the effects aren't immediately obvious.

Mobility is also behind many of the changes in how applications are being developed—although, especially within enterprises, there's a huge inertia to both existing software and its associated development and maintenance processes. That said, the consumer Web has created pervasive new expectations for software ease-of-use and interactivity just as public cloud services such as Amazon Web Services have created expectations of how much computing should cost. The Consumerization of Everything means smaller and more modular applications which can be more quickly developed, greater reliance on standard hosted software, and a gradual shift towards languages and frameworks supporting this type of application use and development. It's also leading to greater integration between development and IT operations, a change embodied in the DevOps term.

Another trend is big data. It's intimately related to cloud computing and mobility. Endpoint devices like smartphones and sensors create massive amounts of data, and large compute farms bring the processing power needed to make that data useful.

Gaining practical insights from the Internet's data flood is still in its infancy. Although some analysis tools such as MapReduce are well-established, even access to extremely large data sets is no guarantee that the results of the analysis will actually be useful. Even when the objective can be precisely defined in advance—say, to improve movie recommendations—the best results often come from incrementally iterating and combining a variety of different approaches.

Big data is also leading to architectural changes in the way data is stored. NoSQL, a term which refers to a variety of caching and database technologies which complement (but don't typically replace) traditional relational database technologies, is a hot topic because it suggests approaches to dealing with very high data volumes. Essentially, NoSQL technologies relax one or more constraints in exchange for greater throughput or other advantage. For example, when you read data, what you get back may not be the latest thing that was written. NoSQL is interesting because so much of big data is about reading and approximations—not absolute transactional integrity, as with a stock purchase or sale transaction.

All this data is also physically stored differently. Just as high-value transactions are processed so as to minimize failures or mistakes, so too is its associated data stored on arrays of disks using high-end parts and connected using specialized networks. But these come at a high cost and, anyway, they're not really designed to scale out to very large-scale distributed computing architectures. Thus, big data is increasingly about scale-out software-based storage that spreads out along with the servers processing the data. We are effectively circling back to a past when disks were all directly attached to computer systems—rather than sitting in centralized storage appliances. (Of course, the scale of both computing and storage is far, far greater than in those past times.)

And, last but by no means least, there is the developer. If we look at some aspects of software development, not much has changed with cloud computing; notably, the mix of programming languages seems relatively stable. However, in other respects, there's a whole lotta shakin' goin' on.

Platform-as-a-Service, as we've seen, decreases the friction associated with writing applications by introducing an abstraction that's more attuned to the needs of developers. In turn, this is leading to new operational models in which developers are first-class citizens and responsible for more operational aspects of the code they create.

But perhaps the biggest change is not in the tools but in what those tools can consume—the application programming interfaces that have become part and parcel of just about every data source, social network, and content repository on the Internet, whether public or private. This is leading to a situation where modular programs and data sets can interact in sometimes unexpected ways as, in James Urquhart's phrase "complex adaptive systems:" systems made possible by large-scale computing, data, and the ability to access from (mostly) anywhere and anywhen.

Into a post-PC world

In August of 2012, market researcher IDC lowered its PC outlook below an already anemic forecast:[53]

> The worldwide PC market is now expected to grow just 0.9% in 2012, as mid-year shipments slow. According to the International Data Corporation (IDC) Worldwide Quarterly PC Tracker, 367 million PCs will ship into the market this year, up just a fraction of a percent from 2011 and marking the second consecutive year of growth below 2%.

Meanwhile, Apple iPad sales continued to skyrocket (especially the then-relatively new iPad Mini). As of this writing, Android tablets remain more of a mixed bag when it comes to gaining buyers, but they'll gain traction over time as well.[54]

Those numbers would seem to lay out the case for a post-PC world rather starkly. Especially when you consider that they don't even consider phones which, in many emerging markets, are the "computer" of choice. Indeed, in 2011, IDC explicitly attributed some of the soft demand to new types of devices. "Consumers are recognizing the value of owning and using multiple intelligent devices and because they already own PCs, they're now adding smart phones, media tablets, and eReaders to their device collections," said Bob O'Donnell, an IDC vice president. "And this has shifted the technology share of wallet onto other connected devices."

However, if you're, say, the major music labels, that sort of growth would be considered amazingly good. Album sales continued their free fall in 2010, falling another 13 percent in what had become a rather predictable year-end accounting. (Album sales actually gained a bit over 1 percent in 2011, thanks to digital albums, and one particular blockbuster—but that was the *best* news since *2004*.) Or you

---

[53] http://www.idc.com/getdoc.jsp?containerId=prUS23660312

[54] As of this writing, Amazon's Kindle Fire tablet, which runs a variant of Google's Android operating system, is the most widely sold non-Apple tablet. And the basic pattern of these numbers has continued.

could be Eastman Kodak, whose core business, film sales, declined something like 98 percent in the last decade.

Against that backdrop, it's hard to call a product class flat to (barely) positive growth passé, at least compared to things that are well on their way to becoming niches even in the near term.

There's a reason for this. Start creating presentations, working with big spreadsheets, or otherwise engaging in many types of content creation and you quickly leave a tablet's comfort zone. These tasks aren't impossible but they are usually a lot easier and more straightforward on a notebook.

In short, the PC is hardly dying even if its growth slows and it stops being the default choice of client device for as many different things.

That said, it's both fair and meaningful to use the "post-PC" shorthand. (IDC now favors the "PC Plus" term, which seems at least equally reasonable.) By way of (doubtless imperfect) analogy, there was once an "Age of Rail" when that mode of transportation was very much at the center of the transportation and economic world. We still have railroads but it would be hard to criticize someone who, sometime in the 1950s, opined that we were now in a "post-rail" world, at least as far as long-distance passenger service was concerned.

For one thing, even beyond sales numbers, I see a huge amount of evidence that tablets are changing all manner of long-held ways of accessing and consuming information and media. At a 2011 Campus Technology event in Boston, iPads were perhaps the biggest single topic of conversation. One anecdote that particularly struck me was the observation that, after getting accustomed to tablets for about a year, students wanted to move away from traditional textbooks *en masse*.

Furthermore, tablets aside, PC-centricity is very much a developed markets view. Move beyond the U.S., Western Europe, and Japan, and much of the rest of the world is centered on phones—both smart and otherwise.

The shift to hosted services from Facebook to Google to iCloud is a big part of this change. The PC as the home's digital hub never really happened in the purest sense envisioned by the likes of Intel's one-time Viiv "digital home" initiative. However, the PC was nonetheless mostly the place where you stored your music and downloaded your software. That hub is rapidly moving out into the network and local devices can increasingly be thought of as "disposable."

Finally, these changes are noteworthy because they have major implications for the vendor landscape. The PC era evolved to something of a monoculture, the stability of which was maintained in large part by an application ecosystem which placed a heavy premium on having a universal (or at least near-universal) processor and operating system platform. That's no longer nearly so much the case in a post-PC world.

Bringing your own devices

The shift away from from the PC as the anchor of the client universe has been largely a consumer-led phenomenon. But the implications are much broader. In business, the new generations of mobile devices —whether phones, tablet, or employee-purchased PCs—are being used with corporate IT systems. The shorthand for this trend is "bring your own device," BYOD for short.

The basic concept has been around for quite some time. But it's usually been couched in the context of a program delivered through an IT department that leveraged specific types of technology to keep the business applications and data separate from the personal applications and data on a PC. It's probably telling that, in this guise, BYOD was mostly touted by companies, such as Citrix, that made products designed to deliver business applications to employee PCs and then securely manage them.

For a variety of reasons, though, PCs—especially in larger businesses —continued to be handled pretty much the same way they always had been. IT usually offered employees a limited choice of company-provided PCs and handled the installation and maintenance of software on those PCs. More and more of those PCs became laptops over time. And the tools to manage those systems improved incrementally. But, in general, the typical approach to corporate PCs in, say, 2010 wasn't all that different from the standard practice in 2000.

But that's changing. For a data point, consider a 2012 report from Forrester Research's Frank Gillett[55] which found that about 74 percent of the information workers in a survey used two or more devices for work—and 52 percent used three or more. Furthermore, the mix of devices used for work was different than what IT provides. About 25

---

[55] http://blogs.forrester.com/frank_gillett/12-02-22-employees_use_multiple_gadgets_for_work_and_choose_much_of_the_tech_themselves

percent were mobile devices, not PCs, and 33 percent used operating systems from someone other than Microsoft.

The vast majority of these gadgets aren't BYOD in the sense of a formal IT program that provides a stipend for employees to purchase specific types of devices. Gillett also noted that: "If you only ask the IT staff, the answer will be that most use just a PC, some use a smartphone, and a few use a tablet." It's something of an irony that BYOD in its original tops-down, vendor- and IT-driven sense has largely fallen flat even while grassroots BYOD is going gangbusters.

Another 2012 report by market researcher IDC that looked at BYOD trends in Australia and New Zealand suggests that more formal BYOD programs may become more common. "Widely publicized and high-profile BYOD case studies are further adding to the peer pressure. One in every two organizations are intending to deploy official BYOD policies, be it pilots, or partial- to organizational-wide rollouts, in the next 18 months," wrote analyst Amy Cheah.

What's perhaps the more interesting tidbit in this report though is that it offers something of a counterpoint to the assumption that BYOD is something that everyone outside of IT strongly wants and prefers. Something that young workers demand of their employers. Cheah writes that "IDC's Next Generation Workspace Ecosystem research has found that only two out of ten employees want to use their own device for work and for personal use, which means corporate devices are still desired by the majority."

Why the apparent disconnect between the apparent pervasiveness of employee-purchased devices in the workplace and the continued desire for IT-supplied hardware? How does one reconcile the enthusiasm for BYOD in some circles with the distaste in others?

First, it's a given that different people have different preferences. Employees span a wide range of personal preferences, salary levels, job descriptions, and technical competencies. That some prefer to just be given the tools they need to do their job and have them fixed or replaced at company expense if they stop working is hardly surprising. Company policies also differ. Some IT departments may indeed see BYOD as a means to cut out an existing cost, others as a way to give the employees who want it more flexibility.

However, I also suspect that the way we use the BYOD term today blurs an important distinction. Whatever the future may bring, in the here and now there are important differences between smartphones and tablets on the one hand, and PCs on the other.

As far as smartphones are concerned, any debate over whether BYOD will or should happen is long past. People mostly buy their own phones and generally use the same one for both personal and company use. One need only look at the financial statements of BlackBerry-maker RIM to chart the decline of dedicated enterprise-optimized smartphones. The only real question is to what degree a company subsidizes monthly carrier charges for an employee-owned phone.

Tablets shouldn't cause much debate either. In their current form, tablets are primarily an adjunct to a PC that can make reading, Web surfing, game playing, and other types of media consumption more natural and comfortable. Some like using them to take notes. Time will tell whether tablets and PCs re-converge in the coming years, but in their current form, tablets can't take the place of a PC for general business use. (Unless they're configured for some dedicated task.) Thus, though many employees do indeed want to connect their tablets to corporate e-mail and networks, they're doing so as additional devices—not substitutes for something currently supplied by an employer.

Smartphones and tablets also have in common that they can be thought of as cloud clients. They don't store much data. They synchronize to online backups (or a PC). They're pretty simple to use insofar as they mostly work or they don't work.

PCs are different.

They can store a lot of files and other data, which will be all mixed together unless special care is taken to isolate personal files from employer files. A variety of products that use virtual machines and other technologies can provide isolation within a single PC for different types of use. However, none of these products has gone mainstream and, for many users, such approaches seem too intrusive for a personal system. Thus, a PC used for work is arguably not truly personal any longer if a company has, for example, some legal reason to examine stored files.

With more and more applications sporting Web interfaces rather than requiring dedicated client software that has to be installed on individual PCs, it certainly becomes more practical for employees to use their own PCs for company work. And for some, that will be their preference either because they want a particular type of laptop or simply because what they do personally and what they do professionally is so mixed together anyway. This requires following proper security practices, backup procedures, and being comfortable doing your own tech support. But it can be a reasonable trade-off, all the more so if the company is willing to provide some sort of stipend in lieu of supplying a PC.

However, I'm skeptical that it makes sense in most cases to have an all-encompassing "Bring Your Own PC" (BYOPC) program. Many people still find PCs (including Macs) to be sometimes confounding and frustrating pieces of gear that develop subtle and hard-to-debug problems. The same people may have difficulty following IT security policies, such as enabling encryption, on a personally-supplied and administered machine. Ultimately, there are still enough complexities with PCs that it's just not practical for IT to get completely away from supporting clients in most environments.

I also suspect that Vittorio Viarengo is onto something when he wrote me that: "It is not about BYOD. It is about SYOM (spend Your Own Money). That's why people like corporate devices."

It's increasingly common practice for people to use their personal smartphones for both business and pleasure, whether their cell phone bills are subsidized or not. And there doesn't seem to be a widespread expectation that employers will start buying tablets for their employees.

However, most companies still buy and support business PCs. I suspect what we're seeing is a certain lack of enthusiasm—at least by many employees—for that part of the status quo to radically change, especially if it means turning a company expense into a personal one.

As journalist Steven Vaughan-Nichols writes: "BYOD is a slippery slope. It started because we loved our tech toys and wanted to use them for work. That was great for executives who could afford to buy the latest and greatest iPad every time Apple released one. But when BYOD becomes a requirement, it's a pain for those in the upper salary brackets and a *de facto* cut in pay for those who don't make the big bucks."

The web app vs. the app store

As we've seen, server virtualization has become a familiar fixture of the IT landscape and an important foundation for cloud computing.

But virtualization is also relevant to client devices, such as PCs. To a greater degree than on servers, client virtualization takes many forms, reflecting forms of abstraction and management that take place in many different places. Client virtualization[56] includes well-established ways of separating the interaction with an application from the application itself, the leveraging of server virtualization to deliver complete desktops over the network (Virtual Desktop Infrastructure—VDI), and the use of hypervisors on the clients themselves. In short, client virtualization covers a lot of ground, but at bottom, it's about delivering applications to users and managing those applications on client devices—including employee-provided PCs as discussed in the last chapter.

Client virtualization is essentially a tool to deal with installing, updating, and securing software on distributed "stateful" clients—which is to say, devices that store a unique pattern of bits locally. If a stateless device like a terminal breaks, you can just unplug it and swap in a new one. Not so with a PC. At a minimum, you need to restore the local pattern of bits from a backup.

However, client virtualization (in any of its forms) has never truly gone mainstream, whether because it often cost more than advertised or just didn't work all that well. It's mostly played in relative niches where some particular benefit—such as centralized security—is an overriding concern. These can be important markets and we see increased interest in VDI at government agencies, for instance. But we're not talking about the typical corporate desktop or consumer.

Furthermore, today, we access more and more applications through browsers rather than applications installed on PCs. This effectively

---

[56] You also hear terms such as endpoint virtualization applied to virtualization on client devices.

makes PCs more like stateless thin clients. And, therefore, it makes client virtualization something of a solution for yesterday's problems rather than today's.

Except for one thing.

Client virtualization, in its application virtualization guise, has in fact become prevalent. Just go to an Android or iOS app store.

Application virtualization has been around for a long time. Arguably, its roots go back to WinFrame, a multi-user version of Microsoft Windows NT that Citrix introduced in 1995. It was, in large part, a response to the rise of the PC, which replaced "dumb terminals" acting as displays and keyboards for applications running in a data center with more intelligent and independent devices. Historically, application virtualization (before it was called that) focused on what can be thought of as presentation-layer virtualization—separating the display of an application from where it ran. It was mostly used to provide standardized and centralized access to corporate applications.[57]

As laptops became more common, application virtualization changed as well. It became a way to stream applications down to the client and enable them to run even when the client was no longer connected to the network. Application virtualization thus became something of a packaging and distribution technology. One such company working on this evolution of application virtualization was Softricity, subsequently purchased by Microsoft in 2006.

I was reminded of Softricity when I spoke with David Greschler, one of its co-founders, at a 2012 cloud computing event. He'd moved on from Microsoft to PaperShare but we got to talking about how the market for application virtualization, as initially conceived, had (mostly not) developed. And that's when he observed the functional relationship between an app store and application virtualization, and

---

[57] In spite of its identification with "thin clients," a sort of next generation terminal, in practice the devices used with application virtualization were mostly regular PCs.

how application virtualization had, in a sense, gone mainstream as part of mobile device ecosystems.

If you think about it, the app store model is not the necessary and inevitable way to deliver applications to smartphones, tablets, and other client devices.

In fact, it runs rather counter to the prevailing pattern on PCs—regardless of operating system—towards installing fewer unique applications and running more Web applications through the browser. Google even debuted Chrome OS, designed to work exclusively with Web applications, to great fanfare. As connecting to networks in more places with better performance improves and as standards, such as HTML5, evolve to better handle unconnected situations, it's a reasonable expectation that this trend will continue.

But the reality of Chrome OS has been that, after early-on geek excitement, it's so far pretty much hit the ground with a resounding thud. At least as of 2012, it's one thing to say that we install fewer apps on our PCs. It's another thing to use a PC which can't install any apps. Full stop.

What's more, it's worth thinking about why we might prefer to run applications through a browser rather than natively.

It's not so much that it lets developers write one application and run it on pretty much anything that comes with a browser. As users, we don't care about making life easier for developers except insofar as it means we have more applications to use and play with. And, especially given that client devices have coalesced around a modest number of ecosystems, developers have mostly accepted that they just have to deal with that (relatively limited) diversity.

Nor is it really that we'd like to be able to use smaller, lighter, and thinner clients. Oh, we do want those things—at least up to a point. But they're usually not the limiting factor in being able to run applications locally and natively. We don't want to make clients too limited anyway; computer cycles and storage tend to be cheaper on the client than on the server.

No, the main thing that we have against native applications on a client is their "care and feeding," by which I mean the need to install updates from all sorts of different sources and deal with the problems if upgrades don't go as planned. And remember how a PC's software sometimes needs to be refreshed from the ground-up to deal with accumulating "bit rot" as added applications and services slow things down over time?

And that's where centralized stores for packaged applications come in. Such stores don't eliminate software bugs, of course. Nor do they eliminate applications that get broken through a new upgrade—one need only peruse the reviews in the Apple App Store to find numerous such examples. However, relative to PCs, keeping smartphones and tablets up-to-date and backed up is a much easier, more intuitive, and less error-prone process.

Of course, for a vendor like Apple that wants to control the end-to-end user experience, an app store has the additional advantage of maintaining full control of the customer relationship. But the dichotomy between an open Web and a centralized app store isn't just an Apple story. App stores have widely become the default model for delivering software to new types of client devices and have certainly become the primary path for selling that software.

The Web apps versus native apps (and, by implication, app stores) debate will be ongoing. It doesn't lend itself to answers that are simple either in terms of technology or in terms of device and developer ecosystems.

Witness the September 2012 dust-up over comments made by Facebook CEO Mark Zuckerberg that appeared to diss his company's HTML5 Web app, calling it "one of the biggest mistakes if not the biggest strategic mistake that we made."

However, as CNET's Stephen Shankland wrote at the time: "Those are powerfully damning words, and many developers will likely take them to heart given Facebook's cred in the programming world. But there are subtleties here—not an easy thing for those who see the world in black and white to grasp, to be sure, but real nonetheless. Zuckerberg himself offered a huge pro-HTML5 caveat in the middle of his statement."[58]

It's often observed that new concepts in technology are rarely truly new. Instead, they're updates or reimaginings of past ideas both successful and not. This observation can certainly be overstated, but there's a lot of truth to it. And here we see it again—with application virtualization and the app store.

---

[58] http://news.cnet.com/8301-1023_3-57511142-93/html5-is-dead-long-live-html5/

The Four "V's" of Big Data

Certainly "Big Data's" most obvious characteristic—and the one from which it derives that shorthand moniker—is its quantity or volume. While we also find the big data term applied to data sets that aren't all that, well, big, there's no question that data creation is a growth industry.

A 2011 study by IDC predicted that 1.8 zettabytes of data would be created that year, about an order of magnitude increase in just five years. That's a lot. A zettabyte is a trillion gigabytes, a thousand exabytes, or 1,000,000,000,000,000,000,000 (10^{21}) bytes. In fact, it's a unit of storage capacity that you probably wouldn't have encountered outside of a trivia contest until very recently.

About 80 percent of this data is unstructured, meaning that it's not stored as a formatted field in a database. Whatever its exact nature, its usually more difficult to process and use than data stored in a regular format or at least semantically tagged in documents. At the same time, it's growing far more quickly than structured data, increasing the challenge associated with using it effectively. The volume and growth rate of unstructured data also aren't well-suited for many traditional enterprise storage systems which were designed primarily with the needs of transactional database systems in mind.[59]

Apache Hadoop is probably the software one hears most often discussed in the context of big data. It was created by Doug Cutting, who was working at Yahoo! at the time, and Michael J. Cafarella. The processing module in Hadoop is MapReduce, which is intended to "simplify writing applications which process vast amounts of data in-parallel on large clusters (thousands of nodes) of commodity hardware in a reliable, fault-tolerant manner. A MapReduce job usually splits the input data-set into independent chunks which are processed by the map tasks in a completely parallel manner. The framework sorts the outputs of the maps, which are then input to the

---

[59] Red Hat's acquisition of Gluster, a very large-scale, software-only distributed filesystem was largely in response to these unstructured data trends.

reduce tasks. Typically both the input and the output of the job are stored in a file-system. The framework takes care of scheduling tasks, monitoring them and re-executes the failed tasks."[60]

Hadoop's complexity can be a challenge, especially when dealing with data that isn't, in fact, all that big.[61] However, because it's structured as a fairly flexible framework, other projects are adding alternate interfaces and otherwise expanding the ways in which the core capabilities can be used. Companies have also started packaging Hadoop and offering it as a commercial product.

Big data is not just about data volume though—whatever yardstick for delineating bigness one cares to use.

Another metric is velocity, a term apparently first applied to data by then-Meta Group's Doug Laney in a 2001 research note.[62] At the time, he was discussing speed mostly in the context of data used to support interactions and generated by interactions on e-commerce sites. However, in many cases, the need for almost instantaneous results has only grown. IBM, for example, notes that "For time-sensitive processes such as catching fraud, big data must be used as it streams into your enterprise in order to maximize its value."[63] Using data in this way stands in contrast to the historical batch mode of data analysis in which a snapshot was taken of production data, the snapshot was analyzed, and a report was created.

Google's Avinash Kaushik injects the caution that the focus should be on what he calls "right-time" data rather than "real-time" data. He notes that "if don't have capacity to take real-time action, why do you

---

[60] http://hadoop.apache.org/docs/r0.20.2/mapred_tutorial.html

[61] Discussed by RedMonk analyst Stephen O'Grady in 2011: http://redmonk.com/sogrady/2011/01/13/apache-hadoop/

[62] Laney's note also introduced the variety term. http://blogs.gartner.com/doug-laney/files/2012/01/ad949-3D-Data-Management-Controlling-Data-Volume-Velocity-and-Variety.pdf (Meta Group was subsequently acquired by Gartner Group.)

[63] http://www-01.ibm.com/software/data/bigdata/

need real-time data?[64] Real-time data becomes interesting if you can get the humans out of the process."

Further making data "big," which is to say challenging to work with, is variety. Unstructured data is often thought of as text—which, indeed, it often is—but it also includes streams of numbers, video, and photographs. Devices such as smartphones are becoming something akin to "accidental sensors" as they snap pictures and encode them with locations.[65] Google's flu trends program takes advantage of the correlation between online searches related to flu symptoms and disease hotspots. Live video feeds create the possibility of all manner of analysis, both for good and ill purposes.

Volume, velocity, and variety—the three characteristics described in Laney's research note—are the most common axes used to define big data. However, one sees a fourth sometimes applied: veracity. This isn't something that applies uniquely to big data. But it's a useful reminder that unreliable data is data that people won't trust to use in decision making. Lack of confidence in data can also be an excuse to abandon data-driven methodologies in their entirety.

And ensuring data veracity is a tough problem, especially when crunching quickly through large volumes of noisy, unstructured, and varied data sources. (Cleansing data can be hard enough even when the problem is much more bounded.) However, it's worth remembering that the ultimate objective of data analysis is to gain some insight that will result in being able to take a meaningful action. And if the quality of the data won't take you there, it's not worth much—no matter how big it is.

Having said all this, there's nothing inherently special about these particular "Vs" or indeed any methodology to characterize data at all except to the degree that it affects its analysis from either a methodological or a technological perspective. And it's even less

---

[64] O'Reilly Strata Conference, Santa Clara, 2012.

[65] http://news.cnet.com/8301-13556_3-20008026-61.html

useful to dismiss real world case studies that don't adhere to some academic taxonomy.

Indeed, perhaps the biggest "Big Data" storyline isn't even about bigness at all. Rather it's about the systematic uses of data to make decisions and take actions whether that data is big, small, or somewhere in between.

Data, models, and insight

I suppose, given the magnitude of the data explosion, the feeling that it must inherently embody great wisdom is inevitable.

Not that this is anything new in the data game.

Probably no data-mining—as we used to call analysis of relatively large customer data sets—legend has been more pervasive than the "beer and diapers" story, which apparently dates back to an early 1990s project that data-warehousing pioneer Teradata (then part of NCR) conducted for the Osco Drug retail chain.

As the story goes, they discovered that beer and diapers frequently appeared together in a shopping basket on certain days; the presumed explanation was that fathers picking up diapers bought a six-pack when they were out anyway. This correlation was then used to optimize displays and pricing in the stores.

That's the story anyway. The reality, as best anyone can determine, is more muddled.[66] The evidence suggests that the project indeed existed. However, the beer-diapers correlation may or may not have been supported by the data. And, in any case, Osco seems not to have made any subsequent changes taking advantage of the purported relationship. That the story has lasted so long probably says more about the dearth of compelling data-mining success stories supported by strong case studies than anything else.

But the vast increase in data volume leads some to think the game has fundamentally changed.

In 2008, *Wired* magazine's Chris Anderson wrote a provocative article titled "The End of Theory: The Data Deluge Makes the Scientific Method Obsolete."[67] His thesis was that we have historically relied on

---

[66] http://www.dssresources.com/newsletters/66.php

[67] http://www.wired.com/science/discoveries/magazine/16-07/pb_theory

models in large part because we had no other choice. However, "with enough data, the numbers speak for themselves."

Most experts don't think it's that simple though. Useful insights don't just pop out of data. You have to ask the right questions. Put another way, there's something of an overabundance of optimism among naive big data proponents that a lot of data by itself is sufficient to solve just about any problem.

Speaking at O'Reilly's Strata data conference in 2012, Xavier Amatriain of Netflix put it thusly: "Data without a sound approach becomes noise." Amatriain also offered insight into how finding the best results requires blending many different approaches, including adding additional types of data as appropriate.

The algorithms stemming from the much-ballyhooed Netflix Prize are actually a small piece of Netflix's overall movie recommendation process. There are a couple of reasons. The first is that the winning algorithms turned out to be very computationally intensive, in addition to being inflexible in other ways. The more important reason though is that predicting how customers would rate a movie, the objective of the Netflix Prize, was never the ultimate objective. That was to deliver better recommendations and, thereby, presumably increase the likelihood that they would remain Netflix subscribers. It turned out that marginally improving ratings prediction only went so far in improving recommendations overall.

Netflix therefore combines personalization, a wide range of algorithms, a huge amount of A/B testing (whereby different approaches are tried with different customer groups and the results evaluated), data from external sources, and even some randomness for serendipity. Data certainly plays a role, in fact a very central role, but it's far more complicated than feeding in the biggest possible datasets and letting the machine learning algorithms churn.

Peter Fader, co-director of the Wharton Customer Analytics Initiative at the University of Pennsylvania, talks of a "data fetish" that is leading to predictions of vast profits from mining data associated with online activity. However, he goes on to note that more data and data from mobile devices, don't always lead to better results. One reason is that "there is very little real science in what we call 'data science,' and that's a big problem."

For example, there's a widespread assumption that personalized advertising is more effective advertising. But a reader's comment on Michael Wolff's "The Facebook Fallacy" nicely summarizes why this might not be the case.[68]

> There is not now, nor is there anything on the horizon, that is a scalable, automated means of exploiting people-generated data to extract actionable marketing information and sales knowledge. A well-known dirty little secret in the advertising world is that, even after millennia of advertising efforts, not a single copywriter can tell you with any confidence beyond a coin flip whether any given advertisement is going to succeed. The entire "industry" is based on wild-assed guesses and the media equivalent of tossing noodles against the kitchen wall to see what might stick, if anything. It doesn't matter whether it's print, TV, or on-line media, no one can predict what will actually work. FB engineers are probably even less well-equipped intellectually than the average ad hack in being able to come up with a better mousetrap to get people to buy what sellers want to hawk.

Other examples come from the talk given at that 2012 Strata conference by Hal Varian, Google's chief economist, who showed off Google Correlate. This tool lets you explore how search trends relate to data—such as time series economic data. This opens up possibilities such as finding leading indicators in search data for various types of economic activity.

Google Correlate obviously depends on access to Google's vast database of search terms. However, Varian's talk also touched on many of the complexities of interpreting correlations. For some purposes, it makes sense to seasonally adjust data, and for others it doesn't. You have to choose search patterns intelligently and you need to use appropriate statistical techniques to interpret the results.

---

[68] http://www.technologyreview.com/news/427972/the-facebook-fallacy/

Google's Kaushik even tries to quantify the amount of energy that should be devoted to applying intelligence to data problems. He suggests spending $10 on tools and $90 on the people who will deal with the data and running lots of experiments. It's all about "scientific method," "design of experiments," and statistical analysis.

Data has value. And, in fact, for certain types of problems insights will fall out of data more naturally than in others. For example, certain types of problems, such as natural language recognition, use so-called "low bias models" that benefit from a lot of training data. Language recognition has also proven stubbornly resistant to more top-down models-based approaches over the years.

And if examples of big wins through data are often still more anecdotal than systematic, they're nonetheless real.

In a 2012 piece in *The New York Times*,[69] Charles Duhigg wrote about how Target statistician Andrew Pole "was able to identify about 25 products that, when analyzed together, allowed him to assign each shopper a 'pregnancy prediction' score. More important, he could also estimate her due date to within a small window, so Target could send coupons timed to very specific stages of her pregnancy." Duhigg then goes on to tell a story about how, in one case, Target apparently knew about a high schooler's pregnancy before her father did.

As it turns out, the events recounted in Duhigg's story are not especially recent; Pole did his initial work in 2002, and it's not an area of its business Target wants to discuss. In part, this is doubtless because it views what it does with data-mining as a trade secret. However, I'm sure it also stems from the reality that a lot of people find this sort of analysis at least a little bit "creepy" (to use the most common word tossed around the Internet about this story).

---

[69] http://www.nytimes.com/2012/02/19/magazine/shopping-habits.html

Sasha Issenberg wrote in a 2012 *Slate* article[70] that "as part of a project code-named Narwhal, Obama's [re-election campaign] team is working to link once completely separate repositories of information so that every fact gathered about a voter is available to every arm of the campaign. Such information sharing would allow the person who crafts a provocative e-mail about contraception to send it only to women with whom canvassers have personally discussed reproductive views or whom data-mining targeters have pinpointed as likely to be friendly to Obama's views on the issue." This contrasts with past practice whereby e-mails were more shotgun and stuck to relatively safe and unprovocative topics as a result.

It's generally believed that Obama's win in the 2012 US presidential election was, at a minimum, aided by a new generation of these data driven efforts. Data's stock was further raised by the widely watched predictions of *New York Times* blogger Nate Silver, whose careful and systematic analysis of poll results proved strikingly accurate—and suggested the superiority of careful data analysis over punditry.

We also see examples from the sciences. Certainly the search for the Higgs Boson at the Large Hadron Collider in CERN is about big data. CERN amassed more than 200 petabytes (1,000 terabytes) of data about 800 trillion particle collisions. Physicist Axel Naumann explained that "most of that [the collision data] is actually incredibly boring, we need to sift through them and find the interesting ones, and even those, we don't see immediately because we can't really tell what we see," he explained. "We can only give it a probability, and so by doing this billions and billions and billions of times, we are pretty certain that we see something or don't see something. … We do a statistical analysis on a huge amount of data and at the end we can give the results."[71]

---

[70] http://www.slate.com/articles/news_and_politics/victory_lab/2012/02/project_narwhal_how_a_top_secret_obama_campaign_program_could_change_the_2012_race_.html

[71] http://www.itbusinessedge.com/cm/blogs/lawson/the-big-data-software-problem-behind-cerns-higgs-boson-hunt/

In the bigger picture, we're in the early days of what sometimes goes by the name of the "Internet of Things," the idea that we'll have pervasive meshes of sensors recording everything and integrated together into feedback loops that optimize the system as a whole. IBM, with rather more marketing dollars than the academics who first coined the concept, talks about this idea under an expansive "Smarter Planet" vision.

We'll only see more stories about great results being achieved by applying data to some problem in a novel way. Especially when there's solid underlying science, algorithms, and models limited only by the quality or quantity of the inputs, more and different types of data can indeed lead to impressive results and outcomes.

But this doesn't mean that bigger data will always hold the key. Sometimes data is just data—noise, really. Not information. It doesn't matter how much you store or how hard you process it. And even when it does hold insight, intelligence will usually be needed to extract it.

The new databases

As data volumes have grown, so too has the interest in complementing existing database architectures with new technologies generally capable of handling larger quantities of data for certain types of workloads.

"Database" had come to be largely synonymous with a relational database management system (RDBMS) or, more specifically, a relational database that is accessed using the SQL query language. Some simpler products run on desktops, but if you are talking about products used for serious business computing on a server, SQL is it. The widespread adoption of open source products such as MySQL and PostgreSQL only cemented SQL's dominance by making it available to a broad audience which couldn't afford licensing fees for products from Oracle or other large database vendors.

An RDBMS stores data in the form of multiple tables related to each other by keys that are unique among all occurrences in a given table. The "relational database" term was originally defined and coined by IBM's Edgar Codd in a 1970 paper. Products based on this database model came to largely replace a variety of hierarchical and other technology approaches. While it could be lower performance than alternatives, it tended to offer more flexibility in how data could be laid out, added, and accessed, cementing its role as a standard.[72]

As computer systems got faster (and SQL RDBMSs were enhanced in many ways), concerns about the performance of the basic approach largely receded into the background. In general, efforts to displace RDBMSs—such as object databases—ended up sometimes generating a lot of hype but not much actual use.

However, with the advent of truly massive scale distributed computing infrastructures, we're starting to see the significant

---

[72] I use the term "standard" here somewhat loosely. While all "SQL databases" have certain things in common, there are also enough differences to make each product somewhat unique, especially when making use of more advanced features.

adoption of technologies which don't necessarily replace RDBMSs, but certainly complement them.

One basic issue is that RDBMSs are architected to process and store all transactions with absolute reliability. (ACID—atomicity, consistency, isolation, and durability—is a set of properties commonly used to describe the requirements.) This is a good thing if we're talking about, say, financial transactions. A bank balance has to immediately reflect a withdrawal; the system has to prevent multiple withdrawals of the same balance from happening simultaneously.

RDBMSs and their associated infrastructure also tend to reflect the assumption that data will be retained for a significant period. Again, this makes a lot of sense in the context of the traditional role of databases. A business not only wants to keep transaction records for at least several years—in many cases, it's legally required to do so.

However, we're seeing the increased use of alternative approaches in large distributed systems which don't have as stringent consistency requirements or which generate lots of intermediate results that don't need to be stored permanently. In exchange, they can use replication for maximum performance and availability.

One form this takes is "eventual consistency," which Amazon CTO Werner Vogels describes as tolerating inconsistency for "improving read and write performance under highly concurrent conditions and handling partition cases where a majority model would render part of the system unavailable even though the nodes are up and running."[73]

Amazon SimpleDB implements such a model. It "keeps multiple copies of each domain. When data is written or updated (using PutAttributes, DeleteAttributes, CreateDomain or DeleteDomain) and Success is returned, all copies of the data are updated. However, it takes time for the update to propagate to all storage locations. The data will eventually be consistent, but an immediate read might not show the change."

---

[73] http://www.allthingsdistributed.com/2008/12/eventually_consistent.html

We're also seeing products that essentially augment RDBMSs by reducing the volume of data that they need to store. An example could be a travel reservation application where the actual "books" need to go into an RDBMS but many of the transactions associated with "looks" can be handled in a distributed way without touching the database every time.

These techniques and technologies don't replace RDBMSs in the way that RDBMSs replaced older technologies such as hierarchical databases. Rather, they trade off characteristics that have been considered non-negotiable must-haves in the realm of database design such as full consistency.

Memcached, an open-source distributed memory caching system, was one early example. It distributes data (together with an associated structure to look up that data) across multiple systems to reduce accesses to external data stores.

We're also seeing genuinely new (or reimagined) approaches to database architectures. A lot of software that is more asynchronous and read-intensive than traditional business applications doesn't have the same constraints, on the one hand, and needs to massively scale performance across many systems, on the other. And for the organizations implementing that software, pairing RDBMSs with distributed data stores of various forms isn't just the right architectural approach; it may be the only way they reach the scale levels they need at a price point that makes business sense.

Collectively, these database architectures are often lumped together under the "NoSQL" moniker which is not so much a description of a particular approach as an indication that a product or project uses a paradigm other than a traditional relational database. As with so much emerging software these days, NoSQL projects typically have open source roots. For example, RedMonk analyst Stephen O'Grady wrote in 2011 that:[74]

---

[74] http://redmonk.com/sogrady/2011/07/06/mongodb-is-the-new-mysql/

MySQL became the most popular relational database on the planet by turning its weaknesses into strengths and successfully leveraging its ubiquity. It was, in that respect, one of the original guerrilla success stories in the open source world.

As the market moves ahead into a world with room for both relational datastores and NoSQL alternatives, we can expect to see patterns from the former repeat themselves within the latter. The most obvious of these, to date, is the degree to which MongoDB is following in the footsteps of MySQL.

It would be foolish to predict the same success that MySQL enjoyed for MongoDB, because the underlying market context has changed. But it is clear that—whether it is intentional on 10gen's part or no—MongoDB is, according to a variety of metrics, the new MySQL.

One of the things that's been most interesting to me is that we've seen so many attempts to introduce new database approaches over the years. We've had object databases, in-memory databases, and others. The outcome has always been pretty much the same. Either the approach turned out to be more limited than advertised or the need was handled by adding features to SQL databases. But NoSQL seems to be the real deal.

As Red Hat's Ashesh Badani puts it: "The movement towards NoSQL has not gone unnoticed. Examples abound of agile development shops and large enterprises alike adopting NoSQL—in greenfield deployments as well as complementing existing application infrastructure. While there are a variety of NoSQL tools available that differ based on the way they store data (document, key-value, graph, etc), MongoDB has been among the most popular with thousands of downloads and deployments in demanding environments."[75]

---

[75] https://openshift.redhat.com/community/blogs/red-hat-invests-in-10gen-are-you-saying-nosql-when-you-hear-cloud

The world of atoms still matters

This book has predominantly discussed a distributed world of bits, of software. But, as we draw to a close, it's worth remembering that "the cloud" is ultimately still something physical. "There's that pesky speed of light" as Lee Ziliak of Verizon Data Services put it as a 451 Group conference in 2012. The context was that hybrid cloud environments may logically appear as something homogeneous but application architectures need to take the underlying physical reality into account.

Latency, the time it takes to move data from one location to another, often gets overlooked in performance discussions. There's long been a general bias towards emphasizing the amount of data rather than the time it takes to move even a small chunk. Historically, this was reflected in the prominence of bandwidth numbers—essentially the size of data pipes, rather than their speed.

As I wrote back in a 2002 research note,[76] system and networking specs rate computer performance according to bandwidth and clock speed, the IT equivalents of just measuring the width of a road and and a vehicle engine's revolutions per minute. While they may be interesting, even important, data points, they're hardly the complete story. Latency is the time that elapses between a request for data and its delivery. It is the sum of the delays each component adds in processing a request. Since it applies to every byte or packet that travels through a system, latency is at least as important as bandwidth, a much-quoted spec whose importance is overrated. High bandwidth just means having a wide, smooth road instead of a bumpy country lane. Latency is the difference between driving it in an old pickup or a Formula One racer.

The genesis of that decade-ago research note was rooted in the performance of "Big Iron" Unix servers and tightly-coupled clusters of same. At the time, large systems were increasingly being designed

---

[76] http://www.illuminata.com/?p=1581

using an approach which connected together (typically) four-processor building blocks into a larger symmetrical multiprocessing system using some form of coherent memory connection. These modular architectures had a number of advantages, not least of which was that they made possible upgrades which were much more incremental.

The downside of modularity was that, relative to monolithic designs, it tended to result in longer access times for memory that wasn't in the local building block. As a result, the performance of these Non-Uniform Memory Access (NUMA) systems depended a great deal on keeping data close to the processor doing the computing. As NUMA principles crept into mainstream processor designs—even today's basic x86 two-processor motherboard is NUMA—operating systems evolved to keep data affined with associated processes.

However, while software optimizations have certainly helped, the biggest reason that NUMA designs have been able to become so general-purpose and widespread is that modern implementations aren't especially non-uniform. Early commercial Unix NUMA servers from Data General and Sequent had local-remote memory access rations of about 10:1. The differences in memory access in modern servers—even large ones—is more like 2:1 or even less.

As we start talking about computing taking place over a wider network of connections, the ratio can be that much greater. More than once over the past decade, I've gotten pitches for various forms of distributed symmetrical multiprocessing systems which were intriguing—but which depended on somehow mitigating the effect of the long access times for data physically distant from where it was being processed. The outcome was rarely a good one. The problem is that, for many types of computation, synchronizing results tends to make performance more in line with the slowest access than the fastest access. Just because we make it possible to treat a distributed set of computing resources as a single pool of shared memory doesn't mean that it will necessarily perform like we expect it to when we load up an operating system and run a program.

This lesson is highly relevant to cloud computing.

By design, a hybrid cloud can be used to abstract away details of underlying physical resources such as their location. Abstraction can be advantageous; we do it in IT all the time as a way to mask complexity. Indeed, in many respects, the history of computer technology is the history of adding abstractions. The difficulty with abstractions is that aspects of the complexity being hidden can be relevant to what's running on top (such as where data is stored relative to where it is processed).

Two factors accentuate the potential problem.

The first is that a hybrid cloud can include both on-premise and public cloud resources. There's a huge difference between how much data can be transferred and how quickly it can be accessed over an internal data center network relative to the external public network. We're talking a difference of orders of magnitude.

The second is that, with the growing interest in what's often called "Big Data," we're potentially talking about huge data volumes being used for analysis and simulation. This volume often presents challenges in and of itself. But, as we've seen, "Big Data" is also about the "velocity" of the data—how quickly it needs to be captured and analyzed—which directly speaks to the matter of latency.

All of this points to the need for policy mechanisms in hybrid clouds which control workload and data placement and for the ability to store data in the most appropriate location across a hybrid infrastructure.

Policy controls are needed for many reasons in a hybrid cloud. Data privacy and other regulations may limit where data can legally be stored. Storage in different locations will cost different amounts. Fundamentally, the ability of administrators to set policies is what makes it possible for organizations to build clouds out of heterogeneous resources while maintaining IT control.

However, policy aside, there is still the matter of physics whether you're talking about the speed of light or the size of a network pipe. Talk large volumes of data and the concept of "data gravity" rears its head. As data gets big, it becomes hard to move—meaning that it has to be worked on in place. Hybrid data storage that doesn't depend on specialized hardware is needed. (Gluster, which Red Hat bought at the end of 2011, is an example of software-only hybrid storage that's oriented towards data that doesn't have a fixed structure, which represents the growing bulk of today's data.)

How applications and their data need to relate to each other will depend on many details. How much data is there? Can the data be pre-processed in some way? Is the data being changed or mostly just read? However, as a general principle, processing is best kept physically near the data that it's processing. In other words, if the data being analyzed is being gathered on-premise, that's probably where the processing should be done as well.

If this seems obvious, perhaps it should be. But it's easy to fall into the trap of thinking that, if differences can be abstracted away, those differences no longer matter. Latencies can be one of those differences —whether in computer system design or in a hybrid cloud.

Four tensions

As with many things, computer technology is often about tradeoffs: performance vs. price, simplicity vs. sophistication, size vs. speed. Cloud computing is no different. In this last chapter, I lay out four tensions that I believe will play a large part in how cloud computing develops going forward.

Private versus public

As we've seen, cloud computing began as a story about public cloud resources and mega-service providers—former Sun Microsystems Chief Technology Officer Greg Papadopoulos' metaphorical "five computers" or author Nick Carr's "Big Switch." In the main, it morphed into a broader and more hybrid pattern, combining a mixture of dedicated and shared resources.

The hybrid concept has been widely embraced by both the vendor community and IT departments for reasons that this book has discussed at length. It minimizes lock-in to any single vendor and it provides maximum flexibility around where data is stored and applications are run. The movement towards hybrid is clear. That's why industry analysts such as Gartner are recommending that organizations "design private cloud deployments with interoperability and future hybrid in mind."[77]

However, a public cloud endgame still has its adherents. Some, like Amazon CTO Werner Vogels (who has referred to private clouds as "false clouds"), come from vendors deeply committed to a pure-play public approach. But it's at least an intellectually defensible argument based on economies of scale across many dimensions including purchasing power, operational scale and expertise, and geographical coverage.

My expectation is that for interesting planning horizons—which is to say five to ten years—hybrid will remain the rule for most medium to

---

[77] Design Your Private Cloud With Hybrid in Mind 24 February 2012 #G00230748

large organizations. The use of public cloud resources will increase but so will the use of dedicated computing resources owned by end user organizations. Relatively speaking, though, smaller companies will increasingly use public clouds, often in the form of Software-as-a-Service just as consumers do today.

Brownfield versus greenfield

Public cloud advocates will generally concede that it often makes sense to leave certain existing enterprise applications running on custom infrastructures in place while putting new applications or functions in a public cloud. In so doing, they're drawing a distinction between IT shops dealing with legacy applications and hardware ("brownfield") and clean-sheet-of-paper architectures ("greenfield").

It's true enough that, without legacy encumbrances, it is more straightforward to adopt a new Software-as-a-Service application or to architect for a greenfield public cloud deployment. That said, brownfield versus greenfield is only one of the factors that go into deciding where and how to run an organization's applications. Functionality, portability, cost, regulatory compliance, performance, and other factors all matter too.

Brownfield versus greenfield does matter in other ways. For example, brownfield drives requirements for hybrid cloud management which can handle a heterogeneous mix of virtualization platforms and other enterprise infrastructure. On the other hand, "cloud-style" Infrastructure-as-a-Service projects such as OpenStack are clearly oriented towards organizations looking to stand up their own version of a cloud within a datacenter they control. So it's a relevant and even important distinction, but it doesn't map neatly to private versus public.

Flexibility versus integration

Vertical stacks were once simply the-way-systems-were-built. This model largely gave way to horizontal layers such as microprocessors, operating systems, and databases developed by different specialist vendors and brought together at the end user. (Former Intel CEO Andy Grove describes this shift in his book *Only the Paranoid Survive*.)

However the "Web 1.0" era, circa 2000, brought vertical integration to the distributed systems world in the guise of so-called appliances, many intended to plug into the network and perform some newfangled Web-by function such as Web serving or video streaming. Appliances promised simplification and optimization but, in practice, they were widely viewed as too narrow and inflexible. James Urquhart noted on his Wisdom of the Clouds blog: "Even if, say, a vendor solution is a 'drop in' technology initially, the complexity and tradeoffs of a long-term dependency on the vendor adds greatly to the cost and complexity."

Of course, it's not as simple as integration "bad," flexibility "good." One of the most successful companies in any industry has famously turned a highly integrated approach into billions of dollars. You may well have a device from Apple close at hand. Enterprises aren't adverse to simplification, either, so long as it gets the job done.

That said, take a broad view of the landscape and flexibility which minimizes dependence on individual vendors seems to win more often than not. Open source is a case in point. Open source projects, although they've matured into solid commercial products in many cases, rarely, if ever, start out as the easy-to-use, just-works alternative. Indeed, open source has a generally deserved reputation for prioritizing features over fit and finish. Yet, open source adoption continues apace, because of its success as a model for development and innovation, while the appliance model has generally failed outside of the consumer market.

Convenience versus control

Cloud computing security and related topics are important. They've also been discussed widely and often, albeit frequently with such a dearth of sophistication that the talk obscures rather than illuminates.

At one level, protecting against data breaches in the data center is a fairly straightforward security problem without many new wrinkles relative to the practices IT professionals have been following for decades. However, in many respects, we are in a place that's different in kind from times past.

Some of this difference is about connectedness and scale. While security models have been shifting from walled perimeters to defense-in-depth since the early days of the Web and e-commerce, cloud-based applications made up of composable services from multiple vastly increase potential attack surfaces. It's a vastly more complicated security problem than setting the ports correctly on a firewall.

Perhaps even more problematic, though, is even determining how specific data and data relationships need to be treated and which laws apply. As journalist Dave Einstein noted in Forbes: "Adding to the uncertainty is piecemeal evolution of regulations governing privacy and data security, which depend largely on where you live and do business. Europe, Australia, and Canada are in the forefront of tackling data protection, while the U.S. lags, leaving a thorny legal landscape for multinational Internet companies."

Some of the issues date back to before the Internet went mainstream. The issues have just become more visible and more complicated. We've already seen big fines imposed for even relatively minor medical records breaches. Expect to read about more fines in the coming year but only incremental movement ahead on the macro issues around appropriate uses of data.

More broadly, we as an industry and we as consumers have probably not really processed all the implications of a shift towards massive hosted and interconnected services. They're much easier and more convenient than the traditional way of building and hosting our own services, but they offer these benefits in exchange for ceding control relative to the era of the distributed PC or earlier generations of the Internet with its more distributed forms of communication and information exchange.

At the same time, a reduced level of control is inherent to network effects and power laws, which tend to lead to centralization. It's also worth remember that, on the Internet, no service is an island. Even if you host everything yourself, you're ultimately connected to the network through an Internet service provider of some sort. There's much work to be done in this area, which includes figuring out just what we want to be in the cloud.

To Infinity and Beyond

My first product, as a product manager, was the MV/7800. It was a 32-bit minicomputer, a "single board" computer successor to the "Eagle" that Tracy Kidder popularized in *Soul of a New Machine*. It wasn't *really* a single board computer though.

You needed other boards made by Data General to talk to basic things like a network. And you needed a Data General operating system like AOS/VS to do, well, just about anything. Wanted to do email? We had Comprehensive Electronic Office—a pretty good product for the time if rather primitive by today's standards. Databases too, whether built to the developing SQL standard or something wholly different like INFOS.

Disk drives? We designed and built them in Durham, NH, hundreds of megabytes at a time. We had tape drives too. The silicon for that single-board computer? The DG-specific stuff came out of a Sunnyvale fabrication plant.

This paradigm shifted with the microcomputer era, which is to say the shift to the PC. The vertically integrated stack blew up, and horizontal integration became the name of the game. As former Intel CEO Andy Grove observed: "Throughout the decade of the eighties, the way computing was done changed, from the old vertical way to the new horizontal way." In principle, the customer had a lot more choice with this model. Choose your components and snap them together. In practice though, the market seemed to favor monopolies—or at least oligopolies—within each layer. Intel owned the processor, and Microsoft seemed to be heading to do the same on the operating system side. Oracle's SQL, at least above a certain scale point, was the last word in databases.

The world seemed on rewind, albeit turned on its side. But it didn't actually end up that way.

In many respects, the processor world did indeed standardize around a single vendor, a single architecture—x86. AMD has competed there against Intel, but with only a brief window of success. The ARM architecture has been more successful with new-style client devices than in servers, but that's a battle that is still to play out.

On the software side, the evolving landscape is far more radical.

Open source changed computing and all that it touches (which is to say just about everything). It redefined the economics of IT and gave control over their software back to users. But the effects went far beyond the source code. Ultimately, open source made possible a style of community-led development that hadn't really been possible previously. It effectively turned what had been a top-down vendor-led approach to designing and delivering product into one that springs from ideas coming from everywhere. Open source development can look messy compared to integrated proprietary products, but time and time again, the choice, flexibility, and innovation stemming from open source have won out.

Furthermore, open source has helped stimulate the creation of the truly open and extensible standards, protocols, and APIs which make the modern interconnected computing world possible. The Internet as we know it would not be possible without open source, and neither would cloud computing. It isn't that the cloud wouldn't have developed as quickly or that it would cost more or not become as functional: it's that cloud computing simply would not exist without open source. The majority of leading public cloud providers rely on open source, and that reliance on open source is permeating many other cloud computing-related projects and products as well.

But cloud isn't just another software development project done the open source way. It extends the idea of sharing code to sharing compute resources, networks, and storage. It recognizes that IT isn't just about the enterprise datacenter—or just about a particular public cloud provider. It taps the wellspring of innovation wherever that innovation is taking place rather than depending on one company's engineering team. It puts users, not vendors, in the forefront of technology decisions and directions. It enables new approaches to developing, delivering, and integrating applications and data across distributed environments.

Open and hybrid are at the nexus of so many central trends in computing. Open in the sense of open source, independent communities, open standards, free to use APIs, and the other characteristics of openness. Hybrid in the ability to move and manage applications and their associated data across a varied infrastructure wherever that infrastructure resides.

Linux as the operating system of the cloud. Developers and applications, its engines for revenue. The data and data analysis explosion and the corresponding need to deal with data gravity across distributed systems. The shift from hardware to software-based redundancy and scaling approaches. Composable software that integrates APIs and services from all over.

Today's IT is fundamentally distributed and hybrid in nature and open source software is increasingly pervasive. Not universal—and there are counterexamples of "walled gardens," especially in the world of consumer-oriented services. But, that caveat aside, the level of interoperability, standardization, and "coopetition" today is unprecedented.

Cloud computing requires bridge building and collaboration across organizations, APIs, and application silos. It's inherently a cooperative endeavor even while the same companies, projects, and individuals simultaneously compete with each other. This is a dynamic in which open source excels. Cloud innovation is also being driven by open source cloud IaaS projects such as OpenStack and even through open hardware initiatives such as the Open Compute Project. Being a cutting-edge technology company increasingly means building on the innovations and contributions of broader communities and other technology companies rather than going it alone.

Cloud computing takes advantage of all this innovation and diversity that comes from open source and from the dynamic community-driven development that open source makes possible. It marries this with new levels of scale and new software architectures that both leverage that scale and make it useful. It introduces new and more flexible ways of accomplishing traditional tasks and makes possible new services and types of social interactions never dreamed of until recently. It intersects with and amplifies essentially all of the big trends going on in computing today from the Big Data explosion to the Internet of Things. It's simultaneously radical and evolutionary. It will have lasting impact—however the details develop and the terminology morphs.

Photo credits

Author photo: Donna Jean Kaiser

The cloud turns on: Don DeBold, Flickr/Creative Commons http://www.flickr.com/photos/ddebold/5113676687/

The shipping container and the cloud: Steve Gibson, Flickr/Creative Commons http://www.flickr.com/photos/photohome_uk/1494590209/

Open sign: Christopher Sessums, Flickr/Creative Commons http://www.flickr.com/photos/csessums/4748225394/

Crane and clouds: Caleb Roenigk, Flickr/Creative Commons http://www.flickr.com/photos/crdot/7321516752/

The Practice of Programming: Alexandre Dulaunoy, Flickr/Creative Commons http://www.flickr.com/photos/adulau/3086751588/

Made in the USA
Charleston, SC
16 February 2013